THE ART OF A QUIET MIND WITH POSITIVE PSYCHOLOGY

A SELF-HELP BOOK WITH CBT TECHNIQUES TO DEVELOP MINDFULNESS, EMOTIONAL INTELLIGENCE, AND OVERCOMING NEGATIVE THOUGHTS

ADELE PAYNE

CONTENTS

Part II
TRANSFORMING YOUR LIFE

YOUR FREE GIFT

As a way of saying thanks for your purchase, I'm offering the book 1 year to Overcome Self-Doubt for FREE to my readers.

To get instant access just go to:

https://upgradebookspublishing.com/free-gift-The-Art-Of-a-quiet-mind

Inside the book, you will discover:

Daily affirmations to overcome self-doubt.

Mindfulness strategies for anxiety relief.

Simple techniques to avoid your anxiety triggers.

And so much more....

If you want to overcome self-doubt and become a social butterfly, make sure to grab the free book.

INTRODUCTION

Talking about a quiet mind, if only you knew, the mind doesn't get quiet in the real sense. It's designed to be active and *thought-full*.

For a layman, it's sometimes hard to track and fathom the amount of traffic of thoughts that goes on in the mind. It makes the mind get so busy and sometimes noisy and restless.

Sometimes in this state, thoughts constantly run in your head, like a never-ending stream of noise. What you'll ever wish for in that state is to find peace, but it seems far away. Just when you try to relax, your mind becomes strengthened. It chatters without restraint.

It could have been cool if the thoughts that flowed through the mind were all positive, but no. Negative thoughts usually find a way of making their presence known in the mind. As much as you try to get free from them, it seems difficult and it feels like you're trapped in a cycle.

If you've been in that state at some point, you'd know that an uncontrolled traffic of thoughts is chaotic. It's just like a mad rush of cars in the evening without a functional control system. It could drive the mind crazy. When a similar thing happens with your thoughts, it takes a toll on your mental and physical health.

Before picking up this book, I sense you've tried different ways to quiet your mind, but to no avail. And the more you try, the more those thoughts keep popping up, even during odd hours.

But what if you stop trying? Yeah, you read that correctly. How about you start all over by understanding the anatomy of the negative thoughts that flow in your mind. The fact is that, when we try to control things we don't understand, we end up being frustrated and anxious.

Striving to stop the traffic of negative thoughts in your mind could get messier when you ignore them or suppress them. Like a high, torrential stream of water, they'll find a way to let themselves loose till you can't ignore them anymore. This could lead to mental breakdown or some other mental health challenges.

But what if you learn to accept those thoughts and observe them without judgment? This might sound like a simple thing to do compared to those "serious" stuff you've tried. But really, it's the persistent application of simple things that usually crack a mountain-like issue.

Therefore, why don't we put aside those complex things for a moment and consider exploring this toolkit of simple skills and techniques that can lead to a peaceful mind daily? Don't get it wrong, a quiet mind isn't the end-game. A peaceful mind is.

As you follow me through each page of this book, you'll embark on a journey to achieving a peaceful mind amidst a noiseless society. First you'll learn to understand the science of your thoughts, the negative ones, especially. And you'll learn how to be rooted in the present, instead of traveling wherever your thoughts lead.

To manage the emotional consequences of the negative thought traffic in your mind, you'll learn a great deal about emotional intelligence. You'll realize that this has nothing to do with how smart you are. In fact, smart people are experiencing mental breakdown, too.

This book is a gateway to mastering emotional intelligence skills. You won't have to react to the traffic of thoughts anymore because you would have understood the dynamics of your emotions and how to manage them even in the most chaotic conditions.

In this book, I'll show you how to deploy a therapeutic technique, like Cognitive Behavioral Therapy (CBT), in managing your emotions. Through this book, I'll guide you on how you can heal broken relationships that resulted from negative thoughts and behavioral patterns. And ultimately, I'll show you how you can enjoy a peaceful mind daily, without having to lock yourself away from society.

Aren't you skeptical about this beautifully crafted solution? Well, I won't be surprised if you are. I was skeptical too when I first learned about them. Don't be surprised, I've had my fair share of this negative thought traffic, too, with its attendant physical and mental effects.

I remember there was a time I went to have a quiet time in nature very early one morning. It was supposed to be a time to relish the beauty of nature and experience calm and peace. Sadly, I left that spot angry and frustrated. Guess what happened? I couldn't concentrate because of unsolicited, negative thoughts.

For crying out loud, who wants to be thinking of an unlikely disappointment while nature is trying to serenade them?

Though skeptical about them, these toolkits you're about to explore saved the day for me. I feel confident about the results you'll get by applying the things you'll learn in this book.

Ready to experience the peace you've so longed for? I won't let you have all the fun alone. Come with me to the next chapter page when you're ready.

PART I

UNDERSTANDING YOUR MIND

What does it feel like when you try to walk through a room full of darkness? I can tell you: it's usually confusing, disorienting, and maybe a little scary. Even when you're familiar with the room, you have to be cautious because you don't know what's ahead.

To walk about with ease and assurance, all you just need to do is to flick the light on.

Your mind is like a dark alley you can't navigate until you learn to understand it. This part is an attempt to flick the light on for you to understand the operations of your mind. It'll free you from confusion and worry.

Why don't you find a comfy position and let's get some light on.

THE ANATOMY OF NEGATIVE THOUGHTS

There is a way to turn negative thinking to positive thinking. It means seeing the positives and not focusing on the negatives.

— BYRON PULSIFER

Negative thoughts can seem like a maze of darkness, with no clear path out. Each turn can lead to more confusion and despair. It's sometimes easy to get lost in this maze. However, exploring the framework of negative thoughts can help us untangle the puzzle.

Let's take a step back. Examining the root of negative thoughts could be helpful in unmasking the strength of negative thoughts. Also, by breaking down the components of negative thoughts, we can gain a deeper understanding of how they work, and how we can break free from their hold.

Your thoughts aren't invisible. Let's track them together one section after the other.

THE SCIENCE BEHIND NEGATIVE THINKING

So, let's say you've had a tough day, and you're feeling discouraged and hopeless. It could make you think things like, "Nothing ever goes my way," "I messed everything up," or "I never get anything right." Considering the context and the emotions you're feeling at that moment, those thoughts might feel true and real. However, it doesn't mean they're correct. Those thoughts are just products of distortions and biases.

Dr. Hannah Rose was quick to clarify in her blog post titled *The Psychology of Negative Thinking* that negative thoughts aren't unique to anyone, it's a general experience for every human. Why's that? Our experiences influence our thought patterns—good and bad.

She added, however, that when we amplify negative thoughts in our minds, than the positive ones, it leads to issues like social anxiety, low self-esteem, depression, etc. However, but don't forget that this isn't unique to you. Those negative thoughts are just being amplified in your mind as they are in the person standing next to you. That means you're not abnormal for having those negative thoughts.

It's believed among psychologists that there's a relationship between our thoughts and emotions. Let's check this out together, what are your thoughts like when you're feeling satisfied? Don't you have all forms of fantastic thoughts, you even fantasize sometimes. No dark thought will stay long on your mind, if it ever crossed your mind that moment.

The flip side of it is that when you're feeling anxious or unhappy, it feels like all dark thoughts are let loose. Your mind wanders aimlessly and thinks of imaginable negative things. If you've been there, what's usually the effect on your emotions? Anxiety, insecurity, or frustration, right?

It was Aaron Beck, a psychologist who studied cognitive therapy in the 1970s, who theorized that negative thought patterns, or "negative schemas," reinforce negative emotions. In other words, our thoughts impact our emotions, thereby creating a cycle of negativity—in the case of negative thought patterns. When this happens, it feels like we're trapped in a never-ending cycle of negativity with no help in sight.

Experts in the field of neuroscience also gave an explanation for the source of negative thoughts. According to them, their study shows that every human has a built-in pattern of negativity. This pattern automatically influences our thinking. This inbuilt pattern makes it possible to consistently focus on the negatives rather than the positives. The name for this pattern is *negativity bias*.

This natural negative tendency isn't all that bad, according to research. Experts believe that it's what kept ancient ancestors alive and helped them survive danger. It kept them alert to potential threats.

But in modern times, things are more sophisticated. There's a high level of sensitivity to many socio-political and socio-cultural issues. This makes the modern era more vulnerable to react to negativity. And it seems the more advanced we get, the more vulnerable and volatile we get. It's one of the reasons this book is timely.

Society's vulnerability is what accounts for the persistent rise in mental health issues globally. Well, if you ask me, I'd say this doesn't spell doom for the different generations that happen to be in the modern age, especially the most recent ones as at the time of this writing —Gen Alpha.

It's just a challenge to create more awareness to reduce the impact of this vulnerability. And also empower people with skills needed to regulate the activities that take place in their minds.

Therefore, by understanding negative bias and learning to challenge it, we can take control of our thinking and cultivate more positive thoughts.

It's believed that our brain is wired to react strongly to negative events, even when they're not actually life-threatening. For example, when we receive a critical email or have a somewhat difficult conversation, the inbuilt negative pattern may cause us to respond as if we're endangered.

This triggers the release of stress hormones. Furthermore, it makes us feel we're under threat which leads to thinking about the potential threat more than anything else. In essence, we're preoccupied with potential threats instead of thinking clearly, often to the point of distraction or dysfunction.

What do you think will happen? We'll likely get stuck in a cycle of negative thinking. That's no good for our mental health.

The effects of negativity bias can be extensive. It could also impact our ability to make decisions. When we're biased towards the negative, we may perceive situations as more complicated than they actually are.

Can you now see the reason why you tend to exaggerate issues when you first look at them? Well, I know this because it has happened to me too. It's only people who have mastered certain skills to retrain their minds that have a more critical, calm, and positive approach to issues at first sight. That can be you too.

But without retraining the mind, our bias can make decision making difficult because we'll be viewing the world through a distorted lens. It's as if we're looking at the world through dark glasses, unable to see the full picture.

One of the results of this negative thought pattern is depression. Study has also shown that there's a degree of relationship between depression and negative thoughts; It's cyclical. Depression can lead to negative thoughts, and negative thoughts can deepen depression.

What a downward spiral that is difficult to escape! In order to break the cycle, it's important to identify and address both depression and negative thought patterns. According to Beck, by identifying and changing negative thought patterns, we can improve our mental well-being.

DISRUPTIONS OF INNER PEACE

Picture a tranquil lake on a still morning, with no single ripple on the water's surface. The lake's surface is like the mind, which can be calm and clear, or turbulent and choppy. In the same way that a lake can be disturbed by wind or storms, our minds can be disrupted by thoughts and emotions.

Imagine that the thoughts and emotions that cause disturbance on the surface of the lake are like the wind and waves that stir up ripples. But even when the surface is agitated, the water underneath the surface remains calm and clear.

In the same way, when our minds are stirred up by challenging thoughts and emotions, we can still experience a deep inner calm and clarity. No matter what happens in the outer world, we can maintain our sense of peace and balance within.

When we go through cycles of negative thought patterns, our inner peace is one of the first things we lose. It can be very challenging to stay calm or find a sense of relaxation when going through a cycle of negative thoughts.

For anyone to lose their inner peace to negative thought patterns, those thoughts must have been consistent and persistent. They can emanate from anything, like low self-esteem, stressful life events, negative self-talk, and anxiety.

We lose our peace when our thoughts get stuck in an unproductive pattern—negative thought patterns. This thought pattern has a profound effect on our emotions and physical well-being. When we're caught up in this cycle, we might feel helpless, overwhelmed, and hopeless.

This makes it difficult to function effectively in our daily lives. When they're left unchecked, they can lead to a variety of negative consequences, including difficulty concentrating, sleep problems, and physical symptoms.

Another way negative thought patterns disrupt inner peace is through a heightened stress level. When you're constantly worrying, your body's stress response can be activated, leading to physical symptoms like headaches, muscle tension, and fatigue.

This stress can also take a toll on your mental health that could contribute to feelings of anxiety and depression. Over time, chronic stress can even impact our physical health, leading to conditions like heart disease and digestive issues.

According to Xi and Lee (2021), something else that disrupts our inner peace are our cravings. We often think we need more to be happy. We crave a bigger house, a fancier car, and more money. We also worry about losing what we already have. But these cravings and worries don't bring us inner peace. They just stir up our inner waters like a rock tossed into a calm lake.

Only when we let go of these cravings and worries can the water become still again. Only then can we see clearly and find true inner peace.

IDENTIFYING COGNITIVE DISTORTIONS

As the name implies, cognitive distortions are patterns of negative thinking that can make us see the world through distorted lenses. These patterns can develop as a response to negative emotions, like anxiety and depression.

Consider this example: someone who is depressed might engage in all-or-nothing thinking. It's a type of cognitive distortion which means that the person might think that since they failed at one task, they must be a complete failure in everything else.

Cognitive distortions also affect how people perceive themselves, their situations, and other people. It influences relationships and self-esteem and they can be damaging to mental health, as well.

APA Dictionary of Psychology (2018) defined cognitive distortion as a "faulty or inaccurate thinking, perception, or belief." One of the examples they gave is overgeneralization. This occurs when we make an ambiguous generalization about a situation or a person based on a single piece of evidence.

Another way to describe cognitive distortion is to say it's an exaggerated way of thinking, and yes, it leads to negative emotions and behavior. Most times, it's not based on facts or reality.

Aside from overgeneralization, there are other types of distorted thinking patterns that you might have practiced at some point.

Let's say you went on a first date which went well. During the date, you had a great conversation and you got along well with your partner. You enjoyed every bit of the time you spent together.

But after the date, the person never texted. This made you start telling yourself that they don't really like you or that they must have had a terrible time. What you're doing is called *filtering*.

Filtering is a distorted way of thinking that filters out all the positives of something or someone and focuses on the negative aspect. This kind of thinking can lead to sadness and anxiety.

Discounting the positive is another type of cognitive distortion that's close to filtering. A relatable example of this distorted way of thinking is when you're working hard on a project. When you reflect on your progress at the end of the day, you recognize a few things you did well.

Instead of being excited by your progress, you quickly dismiss them as "no big deal" or "just part of the job." Doing this restricts you from feeling good about your work, instead you feel like your work isn't valuable or important. This can lead to feeling unmotivated and frustrated.

Have you ever been in a situation where you sent a message to your friend and you didn't get a response right away? How did you feel? And what ran through your mind? If you thought that it's because they're upset with you or they're trying to ignore you, that's why they've not responded, then you're jumping to a negative conclusion without any real proof. That's also a distorted way of thinking.

The last one I'd like to talk about here is called person-alization. I've been in situations where I blamed myself for something happening to someone else. When I sit in a cafeteria that's usually buzzing in the afternoon, with only me as the present customer, I thought I had bad luck that's why the cafeteria isn't buzzing. That's what personalization is.

As a distorted way of thinking, personalization is when people take responsibility for situations that's not fully within their control. It results in feelings of guilt.

None of these distorted thought patterns is good for mental health. They can be worked on, though.

Case Study

During a friends' hangout, Noland shared with others that he struggled with severe clinical depression for 25 years. During that time, he found himself thinking in ways that he had never thought before.

He convinced himself that he was a lost cause and that he was suffering alone. He thought that his suffering was the outcome of his own personal weakness. He never had such ideas before he experienced depression.

He started having these irrational thought patterns when he declined into depression. HIs mind was constantly filled with those distorted thoughts. He struggled to escape those patterns of thinking, but to no avail.

THE IMPACT OF NEGATIVE THOUGHTS ON MENTAL HEALTH

As I've mentioned over and over again in some previous sessions, negative thinking can have profound impacts on your mental health and well-being. It might start out as something harmless, but over time, it takes its toll.

It can be easy to write off negative thinking as simply "having a bad day," but that doesn't fully capture the full impact of negative thoughts. When it's persistent and continuous, it can lead to a variety of problems.

Depression, anxiety, and low self-esteem are consequences of that metal engagement. Do you remember the cyclical effects of depression and negative thinking I talked about earlier?

One side of that cycle shows that the constant focus on negative emotions, such as sadness and disappointment, can eventually lead to feelings of helplessness, emptiness, and a lack of motivation.

This can, in turn, lead to a loss of interest in life and a higher risk of suicidal thoughts. Therefore, negative thinking can be a serious threat to mental health and can lead to a serious decline in well-being.

Anxiety and panic can also result from negative thinking. This is the point where people expect the worst possible outcome in any given situation. This can lead to anxiety with its attendant physical symptoms. When this gets severe, it results in panic attacks, which can be frightening and disruptive to daily life.

Negative thinking can also impact one's self-confidence. As mentioned earlier, it can lead to negative self-talk and a focus on perceived weaknesses, which can erode self-confidence over time.

The fear of failure that results from negative thinking can cause people to avoid new challenges and opportunities. This can lead to a cycle of negativity that prevents individuals from living full and confident lives.

Rapid mood shift is a tell tale sign of mental health issues and it can result from negative thinking. A seemingly minor incident can trigger negative thinking and cause a sudden shift in mood, from positive to negative.

This can lead to behavioral changes, including withdrawing from situations or people. While these mood shifts aren't as extreme as those seen in severe mental health disorders, they're still an indication that negative thought patterns impact mental wellness.

When negative thinking leads to depression, it can further lead to substance and alcohol addiction. When people are experiencing depressive emotions, they may turn to alcohol and drugs as coping mechanisms. Addiction is a very real mental health issue that can cause significant harm.

EXPLORING ROOT CAUSES, TRIGGERS, AND PATTERNS

Our past experiences can have a powerful influence on our current thoughts and emotions. For example, a person who has experienced trauma or rejection may develop negative thoughts and feelings as a result.

These experiences can become entrenched in our minds, leading to patterns of negative thinking that can be difficult to break.

Did you know that falling behind in meeting up with our responsibilities could lead to a spiral of negative thoughts? We all have responsibilities in life, right? And meeting those responsibilities is an important part of living a fulfilling life.

However, when we perceive we're failing to meet our financial responsibilities, it can trigger negative thoughts and feelings. This can be especially true if we compare ourselves to others who seem to be more financially successful.

Responses from people can also make people have negative thought patterns. It's quite easy to feel like you're not contributing if you don't get a response from the other people. This can make you think, "Oh, I'm boring them." or "I must be doing something wrong."

However, it's important to remember that people may not respond for a variety of reasons, including wanting to let you finish your thoughts or not wanting to interrupt. Just because you don't get an immediate response doesn't mean that you're not making a valuable contribution to the conversation.

The physical environment you're in can also have an impact on your thought patterns. A toxic or stressful environment can lead to negative thinking, even if you're generally a positive person.

This can especially be true in a workplace setting where you may feel stressed and overwhelmed on a daily basis.

Your beliefs can also fuel negative thinking patterns. If you have a stereotyped gender-based belief, it'll make you have a distorted view about yourself, like people are not giving you a chance because of your gender or that you're bound to fail because of your gender.

It's not just gender-based belief, there are people who believe that their lack of education or poor background makes them automatic candidates for servitude and poverty in life. They belittle themselves and never aspire for great things.

Usually, these beliefs are often formed in childhood and reinforced by negative experiences later in life. It's important to challenge and change these beliefs to break the cycle of negative thinking.

Setting unrealistic goals can also lead to negative thought patterns. Failure to hit these goals can lead to feelings of disappointment and frustration. It could make you think that you're not good enough or that you'll never succeed at anything.

One more thing about this is that your physical health has a big impact on your mental wellness. If you're not eating a healthy diet or getting enough exercise, it can lead to negative thoughts and feelings.

You might be wondering how that's possible. Poor diet and lack of exercise can lead to low levels of serotonin, a neurotransmitter that is associated with feelings of happiness and well-being. In addition, poor health habits can indirectly contribute to feelings of guilt and shame.

THE CYCLE OF RUMINATION

Rumination is a pattern of thinking that involves dwelling on negative thoughts and feelings. People who ruminate tend to focus on negative events or situations and replay them in their minds over and over.

This can lead to increased distress and difficulty in moving on from past events. Rumination can make it harder to deal with depression and anxiety, and can even make those conditions worse.

Reflection and rumination are similar in that they both involve thinking about our experiences. But while reflection is about learning and growing from our experiences, rumination is an unproductive, negative thought pattern.

Rumination involves dwelling on the negative aspects of our experiences, such as what we did wrong or how bad we feel. This can lead to a downward spiral of negative thoughts and emotions. Reflection, on the other hand, is a more positive process that can lead to growth and a better understanding of ourselves.

Rumination has been linked to an increased risk of depression and anxiety. People who ruminate are more likely to recall negative experiences from the past and feel more hopeless about the future.

This negative focus makes it harder to engage in problem solving and to move on from negative experiences. As a result, rumination can lead to a cycle of negative emotions that can be difficult to break.

This cycle can also affect people who are not struggling with depression or anxiety, making rumination a particularly harmful thought pattern.

At Novum Psychiatry (2023), they pointed out different types of rumination. One of them is state rumination. State rumination is a form of rumination that focuses on the feelings and consequences associated with a particular event.

For example, a person might dwell on the negative feelings and potential consequences of failing an exam, rather than focusing on the exam itself. This type of rumination is more common in people who have a pessimistic outlook, who are prone to anxiety, or who tend to blame themselves for negative events.

State rumination can have negative consequences, such as increased stress and lower self-esteem. Then there's action rumination. Action rumination occurs when we focus on potential solutions to a problem rather than dwelling on the problem itself.

For example, a person who has made a mistake at work may ruminate on ways to fix the mistake and prevent it from happening again, rather than feeling guilty or ashamed about the mistake. While this type of rumination can be productive, it can also lead to stress and overthinking.

Another one they talked about is task-irrelevant rumination. This rumination is a form of avoidance, in which we distract ourselves from a problem by focusing on unrelated thoughts or activities.

For example, if a student gets a bad grade on a test, they might spend time on unrelated tasks like playing video games or surfing the internet, rather than studying for the next test. This type of rumination is not productive and can lead to more stress and poor performance.

And for the last one here, I know a few folks who might be able to relate. It's called post-event processing. It's a form of rumination that involves replaying past events in our minds, especially those that we consider embarrassing or socially awkward.

This type of rumination can lead to feelings of shame and anxiety, and it may interfere with the ability to enjoy future social events.

STRATEGIES FOR DISRUPTING THE PATTERN

Some people who are stuck in negative thinking might actually need mental health professionals to break the cycle. But generally, there are also some simple steps that anyone can take to reduce negative thinking and improve mental health.

I need to point out here that while changing our thought patterns can be a challenging process, it's possible to shift from negative thinking to more positive and productive ways of thinking.

Also, note that these strategies are not quick fixes and nothing will change if you don't engage them. So, it's important to note that to get these strategies to work, you'll need to rechannel the same energy you apply to reinforce negative thoughts to strengthen positive thoughts.

Mindfulness is one of the great tools that I find useful in this regard. By learning to focus on the present moment, you can start to break free from negative patterns of thought. You see, small moment-to-moment mindfulness exercises can be very helpful in shifting from negative to positive thinking.

Mindfulness practice is about being fully present and aware of what's going on around you in the moment without judgment. This can be done with any daily activity, like making a cup of tea, eating a meal, or walking around the block.

Over time, as you become more conversant with being present in the moment for simple, everyday activities, you can start to apply mindfulness to more challenging situations, like stressful conversations or difficult work situations. This can help you stay calm and focused when faced with difficult emotions.

Another helpful strategy is to cultivate gratitude by focusing on the good things in your life. For example, you can take a moment each day to think about what you're grateful for, like your family, friends, or even a delicious meal you enjoyed.

You can even keep a gratitude journal, where you record the things you're grateful for each day. Research has shown that practicing gratitude can improve your mood and reduce feelings of depression and anxiety.

To break the cycle of negative thinking, it can be helpful to practice self-compassion. This involves treating yourself with the same kindness and under-standing that you would show someone close to you.

Who says you don't deserve the same positive appraisal and encouragement you give to others? You shouldn't always be hard on yourself. You can also try using positive affirmations, which are statements that affirm something positive about yourself. Tell yourself "I am worthy of love" or "I am capable of change."

Applying any of this strategy doesn't mean that you ignore your mistakes or look away from those negative thoughts. You have to admit they exist. But instead of judging yourself based on your mistakes or allowing those negative thoughts to determine your perception of yourself, you have to respond more positively.

The trick is not focusing on negative thoughts. Counter the negative thoughts with positive responses and practices so that you can have the right energy to forge ahead with a healthy mind.

EMBRACING SELF-ACCEPTANCE

The first step towards reducing negative self-talk is self-acceptance, which means accepting ourselves as we are, flaws and all. When you practice self-acceptance, you can stop focusing on what you perceive to be your flaws and start embracing your strengths.

This can help you feel more confident and less likely to engage in negative self-talk. With self-acceptance, you can create a foundation for personal growth and improvement.

Now, don't get this wrong. Self-acceptance doesn't mean that you have to love every single thing about yourself. Instead, it means acknowledging and accepting all the parts of yourself, even the ones you may not like.

This allows you to see yourself as a whole, complex person rather than dwelling on your perceived flaws. With self-acceptance, you can learn to love and appreciate yourself more deeply, even if you still want to make changes and improvements in certain areas.

Comparing yourself to others is a surefire way to trigger negative thoughts and feelings. Remember, we're all unique individuals with our own strengths and weaknesses. When you stop comparing yourself to others, you can learn to appreciate and accept yourself for who you truly are. You can set your own goals and work towards your own happiness. Instead of comparing, celebrate what makes you, you!

When you accept yourself, you no longer feel the need to conform to the expectations of others. You can begin to live life on your own terms and focus on your own goals and desires. This can lead to a profound sense of contentment and fulfillment.

Case Study

Abida's perspective about self-love was shaped from childhood. Growing up, she was always told that it was selfish to put her own needs first. She was expected to focus on the needs of others, even if it meant neglecting herself.

It was a never-ending cycle. She felt like she was never getting what she needed from others, and they probably felt the same way about her. But she realized that she can't pour from an empty cup. If she doesn't take care of herself, she won't be able to take care of others.

And so, she started making small changes...

WORKBOOK 1

1. Mention 3 things that usually trigger your negative thought patterns

1. _____

2. _____

3. _____

2. Mention 3 ways you'll apply mindfulness in your daily activities to break the cycle of negative patterns

1. _____

2. _____

3. _____

TAKEAWAY 1

- Thought patterns and emotions are inseparable occurrences in the mind. Negative thoughts produce negative emotions and vice versa. Choosing between negatives and positives influences our overall well-being.
- When people practice rumination, they tend to recall negative experiences from the past and feel more hopeless about the future. Reflection is a better alternative because it fosters growth and a better understanding of self.

Negative thought patterns are like difficult weeds that make themselves noticed even though they're unwanted. They might look difficult to eradicate, however, this chapter has shown that instead of allowing their presence to frustrate us, learning to understand what they are and what causes them is crucial to overcoming them.

Mindfulness is one of the strategies mentioned briefly in this chapter for disrupting those negative patterns.

In the next chapter, you'll learn more about what mind-fulness can do. There are other techniques of mindful-ness, discussed in the next chapter, that can be of great help to you. That's a whole package you shouldn't miss.

HARNESSING MINDFULNESS

Nowhere can man find a quieter or more untroubled retreat than in his own soul.

— MARCUS AURELIUS

I magine you're sitting on a park bench, enjoying the sun and the sounds of the birds chirping. But your mind is elsewhere. You're thinking about a deadline at work, or an argument you had with a friend. You're so caught up in your thoughts, you don't even notice the breeze on your face or the flowers blooming around you.

Many of us have found ourselves in such moments several times. Sometimes, we call it being absent-minded. Let's say this happens during a conversation with someone, they'll know that we're far from them. This can have a negative effect on our relationship with them.

In this chapter, I'll show you how you can train your mind to come back to the present moment, instead of getting caught up in the past or future. The techniques I'll share are practical and applicable to your everyday life.

Case Study

Karen's earliest memories are filled with fear. She remembers the feeling of dread that would wash over her at the thought of being separated from her mother, or of being in any situation where she felt unsafe or out of control.

She recalls clinging to her mother's side, begging not to be left alone, even for a moment. For Karen, the world was a place of uncertainty and danger, and she didn't know how to feel safe.

Karen's anxious thoughts became a constant background noise, a soundtrack of fear and dread that played on repeat. She was always on the lookout for danger, for signs that something bad was about to happen.

Even small things, like having to stay home with a child minder while her mother went to work, could trigger a wave of anxiety.

It wasn't just that Karen felt anxious in the moment - the fear lingered, long after the situation was over. She would replay the events in her mind, going over every detail and imagining all the things that could have gone wrong.

How many other Karen's are out there?

Have you ever had a bad moment that you had to replay in your mind over and over again? How did that make you feel? Would you like to share your experience in the review session or with a friend? I encourage you to do either of both.

ITS ORIGINS AND PRINCIPLES

Mindfulness has come a long way since its origins in ancient Buddhist meditation practices. Today, mindfulness is seen as a tool for finding stillness, reducing stress, and improving overall well-being.

While the practice of mindfulness can take many forms, the goal is to be fully present in the moment, without judgment or attachment to any particular outcome. Rather than dwelling on the past or worrying about the future, mindfulness helps us to simply notice and accept our experiences in the here and now.

Though the concept of mindfulness may feel new, it's actually been practiced for centuries. The word "mindfulness" itself was first used in 1881, when a British magistrate translated the Buddhist concept of "sati" into English. However, mindfulness itself has much older roots in the East.

Buddhism, the philosophy that first developed the idea of mindfulness, began sometime in the 5th century BCE, founded by Siddhārtha Gautama, the historical Buddha. Over the centuries, mindfulness has been an important aspect of various Eastern

Buddhist traditions, like Zen Buddhism, and it has also been incorporated into other religious traditions such as Hinduism and Taoism. In these traditions, mindfulness is seen as a path to self-realization and spiritual awakening.

However, it wasn't until the 1970s that mindfulness first gained popularity in the West. Jon Kabat-Zinn, a molecular biologist, incorporated mindfulness practices into a secular program known as Mindfulness-Based Stress Reduction (MBSR), which was first developed at the University of Massachusetts Medical School.

Today, MBSR and other mindfulness-based programs are used to improve mental and physical health in many parts of the world. While mindfulness was first viewed as a spiritual or therapeutic practice, it's now also recognized as a tool that can benefit people in all walks of life.

Many people have found that mindfulness can help them find peace and balance in their daily lives, whether at work, at home, or in their relationships.

TECHNIQUES FOR ANCHORING THE MIND

When a ship is parked in a harbor, it doesn't leave the sea. But the sea is not one that is stable, therefore, to keep the ship from drifting off, there was an intelligent inclusion into the parts of a ship. It's called an anchor.

When a ship is anchored in a harbor, it's still in the water, but it's held in place by the anchor. The ship isn't fastened to the shore - the anchor is what keeps it from drifting. The mind needs the same technique to keep it stable in the moment

When you create a mental anchor, it helps you to stay steady and focused, even when you're in the midst of stressful thoughts and feelings. It's like an internal anchor that keeps you from drifting away from the present moment.

In this context, an anchor might be something you use to shift your emotional state so you feel more comfortable. It might be something simple like crossing your arms, squeezing your hands together, or closing your eyes and taking a deep breath.

Basically, an anchor is a sensory trigger that can help you shift your state of mind. In a sense, it's a shortcut to a different mental state. You might use an anchor to shift from feeling stressed to feeling relaxed, or from feeling anxious to feeling confident.

But then, anchoring isn't just about feeling positive or motivated. It's about cultivating a feeling of stability and security, even in challenging situations. The goal of anchoring is to create an internal sense of strength and resilience that allows you to face whatever life throws at you with confidence and calm.

Now, what are anchoring techniques that you can practice?

Resource anchoring is a mindfulness technique that allows you to create physical connection to specific positive emotions and states of mind. This technique is like creating an emotional shortcut.

You can instantly access the feeling you need, just by using your fingers. It's a way to harness the power of your mind and body to create the state of mind you desire.

There are three steps to creating a resource anchor:

- Identify the resource you want to anchor, for example confidence.
- Choose a physical cue to represent that resource, for example squeezing your index finger.
- Trigger the physical cue while you're in the desired emotional state. For example, while you're feeling confident, squeeze your index finger.

What you'll notice over time is that you'll create a strong association between the physical cue and the emotion.

Another technique is anchor chaining. It's a mindfulness technique that builds on the concept of resource anchoring. But instead of connecting one cue to one state of mind, here you'll create a series of anchors that lead you from one state to the next.

For example, you might start with a cue that helps you feel relaxed, then move on to another cue that helps you feel alert and focused. Finally, you can end with a cue that helps you feel confident and motivated. This creates a "chain" of positive states that you can access whenever you need them.

Then, there's collapsing anchors. It's a mindfulness technique that helps you replace negative emotions with positive ones. It involves triggering two opposing emotional states at the same time, so that one of them cancels out the other.

For example, let's say you feel anxious in social situations. You could create an anchor that triggers a sense of relaxation and calm, and pair it with your existing "anxious" anchor. Eventually, the relaxation anchor will become stronger, and the anxious anchor will fade away.

CULTIVATING INNER PEACE AND CLARITY WITH MINDFULNESS MEDITATION

Helou (2023) described mindfulness meditation as a way to dive into the depths of our inner world. We're able to explore the vastness of our consciousness and connect with our true self.

It's a journey of self-discovery that allows us to transcend the distractions of daily life and connect with our inner wisdom. She added that as we connect with our inner self, we can find the clarity and insight to navigate life's challenges.

In essence, mindfulness meditation is a powerful tool to help you find a sense of peace, clarity, and self-understanding. It can be a gentle companion on your self-discovery journey. It's a trusted guide as you explore the rich depths of your consciousness.

With practice, it can help you find inner stillness and focus, even in the midst of a chaotic world. It may even lead to profound insights about yourself and your place in the universe.

Mindfulness meditation can be practiced in different ways. One of the techniques is concentrated breathing. You can practice this on your own. Breathe in, and count to four. Feel your lungs expand, filling with air.

Breathe out, and count to four. Feel the air leave your body. Repeat this process, focusing only on your breath. Allow any thoughts or sensations to arise, but do not dwell on them. Simply observe them as they come and go, like clouds passing through the sky. Stay focused on the present moment, letting your breath guide you.

You can also practice mindful thinking. To practice this, let your thoughts come and go, like leaves drifting down a river. Imagine yourself sitting on the bank of the river, watching the leaves flow by.

You'll notice that some leaves are large, some small, some colorful, some plain. They all have their own unique qualities, just like your thoughts. Just simply observe them, and allow them to pass by without clinging to any one leaf in particular. Let the flow of the river carry away your thoughts, until your mind feels clear and calm.

If you're new to this whole practice, you can try guided meditation. You'll need an instructor to guide you on what to do and steps to take. This might not always be needed, but just to get you started.

It provides clear instructions on how to focus your attention and breathe mindfully. This could be with soothing music or a soothing voice. This can be a relaxing and calming way to ease into the practice of meditation.

I'd recommend that you also practice journaling. To get the most out of journaling, consider setting aside a specific time and place each day to write. A journaling practice can be as short as five minutes or as long as you like.

If you're new to journaling, try starting with just one or two sentences. Gradually, you can expand your journaling to include deeper reflection on your experiences and feelings.

INTEGRATING AWARENESS

Developing self-awareness is an essential part of personal growth. By understanding yourself on a deeper level, you can gain insight into your motivations, patterns, and beliefs. This can help you improve your relationships, make better decisions, and find greater fulfillment in life.

It may take time and effort to develop self-awareness, but the rewards are well worth it. With increased self-awareness, you can feel more at peace and better equipped to navigate life's challenges.

Robinson (2021) describes self-awareness as the ability to know and understand your own thoughts, feelings, and behaviors. It's about seeing yourself clearly and objectively, without judgment or bias.

This deep knowledge of yourself is like a mirror that allows you to see your true self, beyond the roles you play in life or the image you present to the world. It's only when you have this level of self-awareness that you can really begin to make changes in your life, based on who you are, not on who you think you should be.

To develop self-awareness, it can be helpful to create moments of stillness and quiet reflection. This can be done through meditation, mindfulness, or any activity that fully engages your attention and allows you to lose yourself in the present moment.

By stepping away from your daily routines and distractions, you can get in touch with your deeper self and gain insight into who you really are. Activities that immerse you in the present moment can include walking in nature, engaging in creative pursuits, practicing yoga or simply taking a moment to breathe and clear your mind.

Inner stillness is a state of ease and acceptance, a place where the mind isn't racing or grasping, but simply aware and open. It's a place of deep knowing and peace, where you can experience yourself without judgment or expectation.

To reach this place, it's important to let go of the need to seek, strive, or struggle. Instead, you can focus on just being present and allowing yourself to simply be.

Self-reflection is another key technique for practicing self-awareness. You can engage in regular self-reflection by setting aside time each day or week to reflect on your experiences.

You can do this at any time and place that feels comfortable and safe, such as at home, in nature, or in a quiet spot at work. In your reflection, try to observe your thoughts and emotions with curiosity, as if you were watching a movie or reading a book.

Allow your thoughts to flow freely, without judgment or self-criticism. The key is to approach your reflection with openness and honesty, as well as compassion for yourself.

MINDFUL COMMUNICATION (WITH SELF AND OTHERS)

Mindful communication is a way of interacting with others with these three principles: rooted in presence, compassion, and non-judgment. It involves being aware of your own thoughts, emotions, and intentions, and being open to the thoughts, emotions, and intentions of the other person.

Mindful communication involves actively listening to understand rather than react, and speaking from a place of compassion and authenticity. In this way, it can deepen your understanding of others and strengthen your relationships.

To cultivate mindfulness in communication, one can cultivate specific qualities that support mindful communication.

- Compassion and empathy: Be open to understanding and appreciating the feelings and perspectives of others.
- Patience and forgiveness: Allow time for understanding, and accepting mistakes as part of the process.
- Gratitude: Recognize and appreciate the good in yourself and others.
- Mindful decision-making: Bring awareness to your choices and actions.
- Self-leadership: Take responsibility for your own actions and reactions.

OVERCOMING DISTRACTIONS

The costs of distraction are not only a loss of time and productivity, but also a loss of creativity, focus, and mental energy. When we are constantly inter-rupted, it becomes difficult to engage in deep, creative work.

Our minds become overwhelmed by competing demands, and we lose the ability to think critically and problem-solve. This can lead to a feeling of mental exhaustion, making it even harder to stay focused and motivated.

In the long term, the costs of distraction can include lower job satisfaction and a higher risk of burnout. Given the many costs of distraction, it's important to take steps to minimize interruptions and stay focused.

To overcome distraction, let's start with a concept in economics: opportunity cost. This concept can be applied to your energy and focus as well as your time and money. When you say "yes" to something, you're saying "no" to other things.

Often, saying yes to everything that comes your way means saying no to the most important things - your health, your family, and your life goals. So it's important to choose wisely.

By saying "no" to less important things, you free up space for your most important priorities. Make sure your *yeses* align with your personal and professional goals. Remember that sometimes it's more important to say "no" than to say "yes." Learning to say "no" will make your "yes" more meaningful, powerful, and impactful.

Decluttering the mind is also an important way of overcoming distractions. to declutter your mind, try journaling. It can be a helpful tool. By getting your thoughts down on paper, you free up space in your mind for more important tasks. This can also provide clarity on any issues that may be weighing you down.

Also, when you find your mind wandering, use the mindfulness technique called noting. Simply tell yourself, "I'm having a thought," and observe that thought without engaging with it.

Sometimes, trying to be complicated and complex can lead to distraction. It's just helpful to be simple most times. To simplify your life and avoid distractions, start by evaluating your commitments and eliminating anything that's not aligned with your priorities.

Say no to new projects that don't fit your goals, and be selective about how you spend your time. By leaving some white space in your schedule, you give yourself breathing room to handle unexpected challenges. Additionally, organizing your physical space and digital life can give you more peace of mind.

EMBRACING JOY AND GRATITUDE IN EACH MOMENT

Studies show that gratitude can lower blood pressure, improve sleep quality, and boost the immune system. Gratitude also improves mental health, reducing depression and increasing positive emotions.

By cultivating a gratitude practice, we can experience greater life satisfaction, happiness, and overall well-being. In fact, studies have found that people who regularly express gratitude report feeling more alive, more connected to others, and more optimistic about the future.

Practicing gratitude is a powerful tool for shifting our perspective and improving our lives. By focusing on what we already have, instead of what we lack, we can experience greater happiness and fulfillment.

Simple moments of gratitude can make a big difference, like noticing the beauty of nature, appreciating a kind gesture from a friend, or simply feeling grateful for our basic needs being met. No matter how large or small, practicing gratitude has the potential to bring us more joy and peace.

Let's look at simple ways you can practice gratitude:

- Notice and appreciate the seemingly little things of life, like the smell of fresh coffee or the sound of birds chirping outside your window.
- Give sincere compliments.
- Be thankful for the things you have.
- Appreciate the people around you for sticking around.

- Write letters of gratitude to thank friends, family members, or even strangers who have impacted your life in a positive way.
- Volunteer or donate

Case Study

In 1985, Anthony Ray Hinton was arrested and charged with two murders he did not commit. Despite having a solid alibi, he was convicted and sentenced to death row. Hinton spent 30 years in prison, most of it in solitary confinement.

In 2014, the US Supreme Court overturned his conviction and he was released from prison. Upon his release, Hinton stated that he held no anger or resentment, and was grateful for the simple joys of life.

Anthony Ray Hinton's story is a testament to the power of forgiveness and gratitude. Even in the face of great injustice, he was able to find strength and meaning in the simple things.

What are you grateful for?

WORKBOOK 2

1. Write 10 things you're grateful for in your journal.
2. Make a note of 2 people who stuck with you and supported you through different phases of your life. Write a gratitude letter to them.
3. Write a gratitude letter to yourself.

TAKEAWAY 2

- Anchoring is an intelligent mindfulness technique that helps you replace negative emotions with positive ones. It keeps your mind stable instead of flowing with the current of negative thoughts. It's in your power to choose your cue and your anchor.
- Gratitude is a powerful tool for shifting your perspective and improving your life. It's as simple as starting with being grateful for the things you have, instead of focusing on the things you lack.

The mind is a powerful part of the human body. It's been learning and developing since childhood. Circumstances, events, environment, and experiences are parts of its learning aids. The first part of this book has shown that any of these learning aids could be the gateway for negative thoughts in the mind.

By understanding this fact, negative thoughts would have been dealt the first blow. And by applying mindfulness techniques, the effect of negative thoughts on your mental health will be reduced.

The next part of this book focuses on giving your life a "facelift" kind of experience. You'll be guided on how to upgrade your emotional intelligence, be more positive in your approach to life, and practice some CBT skills. Take a deep breath and get ready for a *life-lift*.

PART II

TRANSFORMING YOUR LIFE

Usually, the end result of having negative, disruptive thought patterns daily is an uncoordinated and unstable life. Emotions will be erratic. There will be uncertainty about self, abilities, and life in general.

All these can affect one's chances at living a fulfilling life. It can cause some harm to one's mental health and physical well-being as well.

In the chapters sectioned to this part, you'll learn to rewrite the narrative and transform your life by learning and mastering skills and techniques that can change your approach to life.

UNLEASHING EMOTIONAL INTELLIGENCE

We cannot tell what may happen to us in the strange medley of life. But we can decide what happens in us— how we can take it, what we do with it—and that is what really counts in the end.

— JOSEPH FORT NEWTON

For many years, the focus of intelligence was on intellectual and academic achievement, such as logical thinking and problem-solving skills. But emotional intelligence (EQ or EI) looks like a different set of skills. It has different sets of skills, like self-awareness, empathy, and relationship-building.

What really determines success in life and how long your success will last, in spite of all its attendant challenges, is emotional intelligence. This is so because emotional intelligence has a broader, more holistic view of intelligence.

Let's explore the power of EQ to uplift your mental health.

UNDERSTANDING KEY COMPONENTS

Emotional intelligence (EQ) is about more than just understanding and managing emotions. EQ also plays a significant role in our interactions with others (Gitau, 2023). It's about how we communicate with others, build relationships, and collaborate on projects or tasks.

Emotional intelligence isn't just a skill we're born with —it's something we can develop and improve over time. I'd say that this creates a leveled ground for everyone. That's why it is different from other forms of intelligence where some people are born genius and intelligent than many others.

Learning about the skills of emotional intelligence is the first step toward developing it, but it's only the first step. True emotional intelligence requires that you put what you've learned into practice.

In the corporate world, studies have shown that the best leaders understand the importance of EQ and use it to guide their behavior and decisions. Research has also shown that emotional intelligence can have some amazing impact on our success and well-being.

Studies have found that people with high EQ are more likely to achieve academic success, make better decisions, and lead more fulfilling lives. Some experts even argue that EQ is more important than IQ. This is because EQ can help us go through social situations and build strong relationships, while IQ only measures our ability to reason and solve problems.

There are five basic pillars of EQ. I'll mention them briefly here, but we'll learn more about them in detail in subsequent sections of this chapter.

- Self-awareness
- Self-regulation
- Motivation
- Empathy
- Social skills

Self-awareness is the ability to recognize your emotions, thoughts, and behaviors. Self-regulation is your ability to control and manage your emotions and reactions. Motivation is what drives you to go after your goals and focus on personal growth.

Empathy is the ability to understand and share the emotions of others. And the last on that list, social skills. It's the combination of abilities you need to build and maintain relationships.

That's just a peep into what each of those pillars are about. Now let's look into each of them in detail.

EMBRACING SELF-AWARENESS

In the previous chapter, I shared with you how you can integrate self-awareness into mindfulness practices. Let's take a further look at how it is a pillar of EQ.

Just as I've stated before, self-awareness entails recognizing and understanding your emotions and how they impact others. This includes being aware of your feelings, thoughts, and behavior, as well as the effect of your actions on others.

Self-awareness also entails knowing your strengths and weaknesses. It involves being able to question your emotions before you act on them. Understanding yourself allows you to see your emotional state for what it is.

Withtthis knowledge, you can avoid impulsive reactions and make better decisions. When you're self-aware, you can build strong and healthy relationships. Ultimately, self-awareness is a crucial ingredient for being emotionally intelligent.

Developing self-awareness requires learning to accurately identify and name the different emotions you experience. It also involves becoming more aware of the patterns and triggers behind your emotional reactions.

People who are self-aware aren't only able to recognize their own emotions, they can also see the connection between how they feel and how they behave.

As you become more self-aware, you'll find yourself more open to new experiences and opportunities for growth. According to Daniel Goleman, individuals who are self-aware tend to have a good sense of humor. They're confident in their abilities and are aware of how others perceive them.

This is what leads to improved relationships, better communication, and a more successful life overall. Let's put it this way: being self-aware is being your personal assessor. Do it without any bias or pity. Of course, pity will only create a negative view of who you're.

What you should do when assessing yourself is to do it with mindfulness where you won't be judgmental.

Other ways to be self-aware include seeking constructive feedback from others. You can also try journaling, meditating, and paying attention to your thoughts and emotions.

You can also pursue a new passion, reflect on your experiences, set new goals, and use positive self-talk. And one I really love is to cultivate a growth mindset. Carol Dweck wrote a book on mindset, and how it's the psychology of success. According to her, people who adopt a growth mindset have a positive approach to life and they don't accept things as they are.

They don't believe that things are fixed and nothing can be done about them. People who have a growth mindset believe that their circumstances can get better if they're committed to their development. That's one of the profound features of self-awareness you shouldn't trivialize.

SELF-REGULATION

EQ requires not being self-aware only, it also requires the ability to simply recognize how you're feeling. This implies that after knowing what you're feeling, you must also be able to manage how you're feeling. That's what self-regulation entails.

Being able to regulate your emotions doesn't mean that you should bottle them up or keep them hidden. It means expressing your emotions in a way that's appropriate and respectful of the situation and those around you.

You may still feel your emotions deeply, but you can choose how and when to express them. This takes a lot of self-control and maturity. That's why it's a key component of EQ.

Gitau describes self-regulation as the ability to control your emotions and actions. He added that it allows people to make better decisions, even when they're feeling stressed or emotional. With self-regulation, people can avoid impulsive or harmful behaviors and remain calm in difficult situations.

Cherry (2023) also added that self-regulation is often associated with adaptability and flexibility. Those who are skilled at regulating their emotions are better able to deal with change and conflict. They also tend to be thoughtful about how they interact with others.

People who can regulate their emotions are believed to be more responsible and dependable. Of course, no one would want to entrust anything worthwhile to someone who is emotionally unstable. No one would trust them to go through with their work because anything could trigger their mood to swing at any time.

So, how do you regulate your emotions?

To regulate your emotions, it sure starts with being aware of them, right? Afterwards, it's also important to build distress tolerance skills and find healthy ways to cope with stress and anxiety.

Learning to regulate your emotions also requires that you constantly practice effective communication skills. This also includes that you have to recognize that you have a choice in how you respond to situations.

Also, learn to practice cognitive reframing. This means that you consciously change negative thought patterns to positive ones. It'll help you regulate your emotions. Don't forget that thoughts influence emotions and vice-versa. Negative thoughts will produce negative emotions. That's why you need to see things from a positive perspective.

Also, learn to accept your emotions, both negative and positive. Instead of ignoring or denying them, embrace them. Accepting them helps us to manage them better in a healthy way.

EMPATHY

The first two components I discussed focuses on self—understanding yourself and managing yourself. However, as a component of EQ, empathy makes you look outward. Empathy allows you to understand and relate to the emotions of others. But of course, you can't do this without having a hang of your emotions first.

Empathy is the ability to put yourself in someone else's shoes. This is essential for healthy relationships because it helps build trust and connection. Through empathy you can recognize and go through various social dynamics that exist between different individuals and groups.

This knowledge helps build better relationships and have more productive interactions with others, even when you come from different cultural or social backgrounds. Empathy fosters mutual respect and understanding, which are crucial for social harmony.

In essence, an important part of empathy is understanding and respecting diversity, as well as practicing active listening and clear communication. It's important to pay close attention to both verbal and nonverbal cues, such as body language, to fully understand the emotional states of others.

In the workplace' context, empathy allows you to understand and connect with your team on a deeper level. If you're empathetic as a leader, your employees will feel supported and valued, which leads to increased engagement and productivity. This, in turn, creates a more positive and harmonious work environment.

Cherry (2023) believes that individuals with a high level of empathy are skilled at discerning power dynamics in interpersonal relationships. They can recognize who holds power in a given situation and understand how that affects each person's emotions and behavior.

Ready to nurture empathy?

First, try to be open and honest about your feelings. Don't hide it. But also, it has to be done in a safe environment where someone won't take advantage of you. Next, find something you're passionate about and get involved. It could be a community project, a family event, a class activity, or even hang out with friends. Be involved.

Also, make some effort to actively listen to others. It doesn't have to be about you. This doesn't have to be about your personality trait—introvert or extrovert. Actively listening is beyond just hearing what the other person is saying, you're also showing undivided interest in what they're saying such that the other person will know you're truly listening. You can start practicing active listening by talking to new people.

Another way to practice empathy is to put yourself in someone else's shoes and imagine what it would be like to be them. It would shape your perspective about them and enable you to interact with them with more compassion.

BUILDING SOCIAL SKILLS

It's important to know that empathy is more than just understanding the emotions of yourself and others. It's about applying that understanding in your daily life and relationships.

You need to be able to use your emotional intelligence to communicate effectively, build trust, and resolve conflict. Without this practical application, emotional understanding is just a concept, not a skill.

Therefore, the ability to effectively communicate, resolve conflicts, and build relationships is known as social skills—another component of EQ. It allows you to handle challenging social interactions.

With strong social skills, you can articulate your ideas clearly, connect with others, and find solutions to disagreements. Just imagine what it would feel like to apply this to a professional space.

In a professional space, leaders with strong social skills are often well-liked and well-respected by their team members. They're approachable, easy to talk to, and make their teams feel comfortable and valued.

This builds trust and rapport, which in turn leads to more effective teamwork and communication. Additionally, social skills help leaders to be more persuasive, as they're able to understand and connect with others. It makes them better able to convince people to see their point of view and get on board with their ideas.

Employees also benefit from these skills. Employees who are able to build strong relationships with their managers and colleagues are often happier and more engaged in their work. They feel more connected to their team and have a stronger sense of belonging.

How effective do you think they'll be at work?

You guessed right. They'll be more productive, creative, and satisfied at their workplace.

So, how can you go about this?

When developing social skills, it's important that you learn to ask open-ended questions. It'll encourage others to share their thoughts and ideas. It'll also help you understand their perspective.

Also, it's important to pay attention to the social skills of others. By observing how they communicate, you can learn new strategies for improvising yours. Then try to maintain good eye contact during conversations. It could be difficult, right? I can relate. But if you can learn to do this, it'll create a level of connection between you and others. It'll also indicate that you're interested and engaged in the conversation.

Also learn to show genuine interest in others. This means you listen closely to them, ask them thoughtful questions, and pay close attention to their responses. You can do this by using "icebreakers" to start the conversations. Icebreakers are simple questions or comments that break the ice and help to establish a connection.

For example, you could ask someone about their hobbies or interests, or share something about yourself that they might find interesting. You could also thoughtfully drop in on people occasionally just to check in on them. This shows that you care about them and their well-being, and it helps to build trust.

You can also use this time to ask how they're doing and offer any support or help if needed. This will make them feel valued and appreciated. It's a key to establishing strong social skills.

Another valid way of building social skills is being sensitive to the needs of others. This would definitely require a level of empathy. However, it's a way to build social connections.

For instance, if someone seems upset or stressed, you could offer them a listening ear or a word of encouragement. By being sensitive to their needs, you can build strong relationships and make them feel supported.

EI IN PERSONAL AND PROFESSIONAL SUCCESS

While discussing the components of emotional intelligence in the previous section, I made reference to their application in the professional settings. Let's take that a step further.

Personal success in this context refers to how EI or EQ skills could help you succeed at a personal level, maybe in achieving a personal health, relationship, or career goal. Professionally, it's considering how these skills can help you to be more productive and efficient in your workplace.

I understand that there's a lot of toxicity in many workplaces. However, you can choose to be different. Toxicity in workplaces is one of the reasons for the rise in the level of negativity in many societies today.

An APA survey revealed that workplace mental health is a growing concern. A significant portion of workers reported experiencing harm to their mental health at work (Bethune, 2023). 1 in 5 said they experienced harassment in the past year. Apart from affecting workers' efficiency at work, it could make them toxic and negative as well.

However, employers who are invested in supporting the mental health of their workers, according to this survey, will have a better yearly turnover and great team to work with. Thus, introduction of EI skills at every organization is crucial for professional success.

On a personal level, EI can help you build stronger relationships, manage stress, increase your resilience, make better decisions, and foster effective communications. We discussed this in the previous section.

In the workplace, EI can lead to improved communication, teamwork, and leadership skills. It also leads to increased job satisfaction, greater influence and persuasiveness, and enhances problem-solving and conflict resolution.

Overall, EI can have a significant impact on your personal development and well-being. It'll increase your self-awareness and emotional regulation skills. You'll be able to lead a more fulfilling and satisfying life.

In addition, for professional success, EI helps you communicate effectively, work as part of a team, and handle complex situations without breaking a sweat. This is great for building a great work culture, especially with the upsurge in the gig economy, where there's no definitive work policy yet or some benefits onsite workers enjoy.

EI AND RESILIENCE

One of the things Goleman said about EQ was that it can help people cope with and recover from crisis situations. He said all those components of EQ, which we already discussed, can give people the strength and resilience they need to overcome challenges and thrive in difficult times.

People with high EI are better equipped to handle the emotional demands of stressful situations. They're able to accurately perceive and evaluate their own emotions. They know when to express them and how. They can regulate their moods.

This is to say that emotionally intelligent people are more resilient and adaptable when facing adversity. When you see emotionally resilient people you'll notice that they're highly self-aware of their emotions and believe they have the ability to manage the challenges life throws at them.

This self-confidence allows them to adapt and cope with crises. So, instead of feeling overwhelmed or hopeless, they're optimistic and determined to see the end of the crises. Instead of bowing their heads in defeat and self-pity, they raise their heads high to square up against their challenges. They don't allow situations to control their mood, they set it.

It's not just the components of EI that reinforce resilience. The support and encouragement we get from our social networks also help us develop resilience. You know empathy helps us build strong and supportive relationships, right?

Now, the people we've successfully built a relationship with can turn out to become our support system. They can be valuable resources when we need to bounce back from adversity.

So, sharing our emotions and experiences with others —a way to cultivate social skills—can help us feel connected and supported. This can give us the confidence and strength to face challenges head-on.

One other way resilience is built is having a positive outlook. When you see opportunities in challenges, and have a sense of optimism, you're likely to stand your ground resiliently when situations are unpleasant.

By adopting these attitudes, you can maintain a sense of hope and motivation even when facing difficult circumstances.

One common thing between EI and resilience is that both skills enhances the ability to adapt. EI equips people with the social skills and empathy needed to adapt to others' needs and emotions. Resilience also enables people to adapt to change and find creative solutions.

In other words, these skills are linked. Together, they help people handle the hurdles of life with grace and flexibility.

Case study

Around 2013, Detroit was faced with economic hardship. There was massive loss of jobs and a huge reduction in its population. Buildings were crumbling and the signs of poverty were palpable.

In the midst of this, an African American man in his forties chose how to view the situation. He was homeless and had just got out of jail after serving a sentence for assault.

The man had taken responsibility for his actions and felt remorse for what he had done. But reflecting over his life, he felt like a different man and was determined to stay out of trouble. Eventually, he managed to get a job that paid $13 per hour. He was grateful for the opportunity and felt hopeful about the future.

Now, that's resilience, don't you think so too? In your view, how did this American demonstrate resilience?

ENHANCING EQ IN EVERYDAY LIFE

Can I practice EQ in my daily life?

Of course! That's the goal my friend. There are different ways you can practice EQ daily. Being able to accept criticism without being embittered is one important way. It shows that you've gained control over your emotions, you have a positive outlook, and a growth mindset.

Another way is to take responsibility for your actions. When things go wrong or when we're criticized, it's easy to become defensive or blame others, isn't it? However, taking feedback and owning up to our mistakes show emotional maturity and resilience.

You can also practice EQ daily through what you do after taking responsibility for your mistake. Do you move on or you ruminate on it?

Ability to move on after making mistakes is a great way to demonstrate EQ daily. We all make mistakes, don't we? But dwelling on them and beating ourselves up only creates negative emotions and doesn't help us grow. Instead, we can learn from our mistakes and move forward.

Ability to say "no" is another way to demonstrate EQ daily. Saying no can be hard, especially if you're worried about disappointing others or being seen as selfish. However, it's important to set boundaries and prioritize your needs. If you don't, you may end up feeling resentful and burnt out.

You can also demonstrate EQ daily through how you share your feelings. You can do it in a healthy and respectful way, you know? This includes expressing feelings like anger, sadness, and joy in a way that is constructive, rather than destructive. It also involves listening and validating the feelings of others.

Before I conclude this chapter, I'd like to emphasize that EQ isn't something you master in one day, it's a process of consistent practice. You can actually commit yourself to practicing EQ daily.

Don't get discouraged if you're not getting it right yet. Keep trying and be your first cheer leader. You could also get the motivation to keep trying in your support group as well. The goal is to be emotionally intelligent.

Case Study

Anthony, the CEO of a growing company, found the staff meetings every two months to be tiresome and ineffective. The meetings were open to all employees, who used the opportunity to air numerous grievances and complaints, many of which were repetitive.

While Anthony tried to maintain a cheerful attitude, his mind would switch off during the meetings. However, as a result of the issues the employees complained about, the company started losing employees. Anthony couldn't salvage it.

WORKBOOK 3

1. In what ways could EQ have saved Anthony's company in the story above?

_____

_____

_____

2. Resilience exercise: Identify and note down any task you abandoned some time ago. Revisit the task. Write out a plan on how to handle the task again. Define how long you'll do it. Then get started.

TAKEAWAY 3

- EQ is uniquely different from IQ because it isn't inborn. However, EQ can be cultivated and nurtured through learning and practice.
- EQ skills are not limited to the classroom and specific places. It's useful for all life's endeavors. It determines the span of life, relationships, and position at work.

EQ is a great tool to achieve emotional stability and correction of perspective. With the application of the components of EQ, people can take charge of their emotions, thus their lives, to become better people in their family, community, and at work.

While EQ lays the foundation for having a positive outlook on life, there's a way to persistently live with this positive mindset. It's the key to happiness. You'll find this key in the next chapter.

4

INTEGRATING POSITIVE PSYCHOLOGY PRINCIPLES

The greatest discovery of my generation is that human beings can alter their lives by altering their attitudes of mind.

— WILLIAM JAMES

Previously, we learned about the inbuilt negative patterns at play in our minds. Any step to disrupt that pattern is counter-bias training. It won't come on a platter because it's like going against a strong tide.

It'll require some conscious efforts and persistent willingness to continue with the effort without backing down regardless of the challenges. I'm about to take you through some counter-bias training to replace negative thought patterns with positive ones. The objective is for you to learn how to adopt new thought patterns that help you focus on the good rather than the bad.

Case Study

Ben and Alex were brothers in high school. Ben was two years younger than Alex who was 17. Between the two, Ben was the optimistic one. He had a positive outlook on life. Alex on the other hand was a bit of a worrier.

Ben experienced life as an adventurer. Alex couldn't help but expect the worst. During Alex's final year in high school, their dad was diagnosed with terminal bone cancer. The whole family went through a lot of pain, sleepless nights, treatments, and tears. They never lost hope, but they said their goodbyes in due time.

When the funeral took place, the family returned home, receiving visitors who were paying their respects. Alex was sitting next to his mom, crying, feeling hopeless, unable to speak. It was as though all life could offer was suffering.

To worsen the situation for Alex, his little brother, Ben, seemed unfazed by the entire occurrence. This made Alex angrier. Ben was somewhere in the room welcoming visitors, giving them little talks, serving them coffee and cookies, smiling, and acting as though everything was normal.

Alex wondered how Ben could be so unbothered by the loss of their father. He wondered if Ben was just pretending, trying to hide his grief.

Wouldn't you have reacted like Alex if Ben were your brother?

What made Ben react differently than Alex? You're about to find out.

THE SCIENCE OF POSITIVE PSYCHOLOGY

In the 1950s, Psychologist Abraham Maslow coined the term, "Positive Psychology." While the field of psychology at the time focused on mental illness, Maslow believed that the study of human behavior should also consider people's potential for personal growth and fulfillment. This opened up the field to a new field of learning.

It was later, other humanistic psychologists like Carl Rogers built on Maslow's work. They contributed to the ideas that helped shape the emerging field of Positive psychology. This field of study has since expanded to include a diverse range of topics, from happiness and well-being to motivation and flourishing.

Years later, Martin Seligman, the former President of the American Psychological Association (APA), popularized the term "Positive Psychology" with his book, *Authentic Happiness*. That's where he defined the field as the study of positive emotions and the strengths that help individuals and communities thrive.

According to Ackerman (2018), it's important to note that positivity psychology is actually based on some intense science and research. It's a subfield of psychology, and while it has sometimes been dismissed as being too "soft" or "pseudoscientific," it uses the same scientific methods as other branches of psychology.

Theories are tested and evaluated based on the available evidence, and the field is constantly evolving to incorporate new findings.

In the words of a University of Michigan professor and positive psychologist, Peterson (2008), positive psychology isn't the same as untested self-help or unfounded affirmations. It's not to be confused with secular religion either. No matter how good these things might make us feel, they're not science.

According to him, positive psychology is a science, not a recycled version of the power of positive thinking or the secret. And to expand the thought of the founding father of this field, Seligman, the aim of positive psychology is to move away from the study of illness and mental disorders, and instead focus on the positive aspects of the human experience—what makes life worth living.

It's about finding ways to build resilience, develop personal strengths, and foster well-being. In other words, it's about promoting health rather than treating disease. It's a bid to shift psychology's focus from darkness to light.

SHIFTING FOCUS FROM NEGATIVE TO POSITIVE

Speaking about shifting from darkness to light, negative to positive, it's an effort to train the mind to view the world in a different way. It emphasizes the positive aspects of life rather than the negatives.

The goal is to change the way we think about ourselves and our circumstances. It's an effort to help us overcome negative thinking patterns and focus on the good in our lives. Without doubt, this process will take time and effort. But it comes with transformational rewards.

Do you remember how things are when you focus on negatives? You dwell more on things that have gone wrong in your life, the mistakes you've made, or the things you don't like about yourself.

Now, retraining your mind means that you're training your mind to adopt a new, positive perspective about yourself. It'll change your perspective to focus on the things that are going right, the things you've accomplished, and the things you like about yourself.

It's also a way to see the world in a different light. You'll focus on the beauty and possibilities instead of the ugliness and negativity. Isn't that something you'd like to do?

But hold that thought for a while. Whenever you catch yourself thinking, "Is there anything good in life to be happy about?" That's exactly the reason why you need a shift in your perspective.

No matter how ugly your experiences are, there's still something good about your life. You just have to try looking again. This time, remove the distorted lens of negativity and steer your mind away from negative thoughts.

Come to think of it, if your life had been all bad, you wouldn't have a dime to give you access to this book. You won't even be able to read to this point. There's still something to be grateful for in your life. That's something positive.

Don't forget that the reason why you need to shift your focus to positive things is that it uplifts your emotions and mental well-being. Remember that emotions and thoughts are cyclical in their operations, right? One affects the other.

I'm sure you don't want to live in depression and gloominess all your life. Therefore, make some effort to shift your focus from what's not been going well and focus on the good things of your life. You'll be amazed at what you'll find.

One of the ways you can shift your focus is by practicing mindful awareness. It's the process of focusing on the present moment and observing your thoughts without judgment. It's one of the ways you can begin to identify negative thought patterns and consciously shift your focus to the positive.

Another strategy you can deploy is reframing. Reframing is the process of taking a negative thought or situation and looking at it from a different, more positive perspective.

Let's say you're stuck in traffic and feel frustrated, you could reframe the situation by focusing on the fact that you're getting some extra time to listen to your favorite music or audiobook.

Another strategy is gratitude. Gratitude requires a degree of thoughtfulness and reflection. Through these skills, you'll identify things and people that you should be grateful for. When people complain and grumble a lot, it's because they're focusing on things that are not working.

Gratitude shifts your focus to see things that are working. You'll identify things you've achieved in the past and things you possess. Learn to be grateful even during unpleasant times. Do you know why? Locked within unpleasant times are opportunities for innovative solutions.

CULTIVATING POSITIVE EMOTIONS

Just like a farmer tills the ground to get the soil ready for cultivating a plant, everything we've spoken about until this point was to prepare your mind to nurture positivity. Positive emotions can be cultivated.

Using a farmer as an example again. A land that's left unattended to will have weeds grow on it. Your mind doesn't need to invite negative thoughts, they just plant themselves in there. But just as a farmer will diligently work to raise a new kind of plant on the same land, you'll need to do the same for your mind.

Cultivating positivity takes work. Great thing is, you don't have to do it alone. I've taken the first step by putting this book together for you. What you need to do is just to follow the methods and techniques. And while you're doing that, I'll keep cheering you on. Then you also have your support groups too.

I'd need to say that there are no hard fast rules to cultivating positive emotions. However, there are common, general things I could ask you to do just to guide you to get started. Since the goal is to achieve happiness, the things that make people happy differ from person to person. I'll guide you to identify yours. In the end, cultivating positive emotions is only a means to that end.

But that also means that the actions have to be positive as well. I had to say that because there are folks who derive "happiness" from hurting other people. That's no positive action, right? So, everything we're saying here is founded on positivity.

Let's start cultivating positive emotions by identifying the things already bringing you happiness. Those activities can be clues to the direction you want to take to increase positivity in your life.

Let's assume that you like gardening or listening to music. Either of these can be a good starting point for developing a positive mindset. Afterwards, try adding other activities that have even proven to have positive emotional effects on you, such as exercise, meditation, or spending time with friends.

Be compassionate to yourself. It breeds positive emotions. You'll remember that self-compassion is the practice of treating yourself with the same kindness and understanding you would show to a friend.

Recognize and accept your flaws and mistakes without judgment or shame. However, don't condone them. Those are two different things. Recognizing and accepting them would make you forgive yourself and tell yourself you could do better instead of condemning yourself.

But condoning your flaws and mistakes is to admit that there's nothing wrong in what you're doing and you're likely to willfully do it again. That's not what self-compassion is about.

Self-compassion releases you from negative thoughts and self-criticism that can weigh you down. This leads to emotional growth, healthier self-image, and a more positive outlook on life.

Acts of kindness can also help you cultivate positive emotions. To start with, it takes a generous mind to extend kindness to other people. And I tell you, that's so positive! A lot of things go into play before acting kindly. Empathy is one of them. Acting kindly combines components of EQ to get done.

The more you practice them, the more you nurture positive emotions. Gratitude, mindfulness meditation, and physical exercises are also ways you can nurture positive emotions.

THE POWER OF POSITIVE THINKING

Positive mindset—positive thinking—is one of the greatest forces that makes things happen and get things done. You might be wondering how that's possible. But yeah, believing that it's possible is positive, and it's powerful enough to make you experience the greatest transformation you desire.

There's something about thinking positively that medical science also attests to. A study from the University of Sydney showed a link between optimism and faster recovery from illness, including cancer.

The study's lead researcher, Professor Donnel Briley, stated that patients who are optimistic about their recovery when ill, are more likely to recover. While more research is needed to understand the impact of optimism on healing, this study provides evidence that a positive attitude can have physical health benefits.

Research has also suggested that happier patients may have a better chance of achieving a positive outcome. While the reasons for this aren't fully understood yet, some experts suggest that optimism and positive thinking may boost immunity and help the body to heal. It may also reduce stress levels and promote better sleep and overall well-being.

Andrade (2019) also stated that in order to achieve goals and live happily, we must consistently focus on positive thoughts and try to avoid negative thoughts. He shared ways to do that.

He said that when we visualize success, repeat positive affirmations, and speak positively to ourselves it builds self-esteem. Also, focusing on happy thoughts helps to minimize stress. You can do this despite the negativity around you.

There's growing evidence to suggest that positive thinking can have a significant impact on our physical and mental health. Studies have shown that optimistic people tend to have lower rates of depression and anxiety and they also have a reduced risk of developing serious health conditions like heart disease and stroke.

Optimism has even been linked to a lower risk of dying from certain illnesses. Additionally, it has been shown to increase pain tolerance and improve the outcomes of patients with certain conditions.

An expert at John Hopkins, Lisa R. Yanek found that people with a family history of heart disease who maintain a positive outlook on life are significantly less likely to develop heart disease themselves.

The study showed that people with a family history of heart disease, those who had an optimistic outlook were 33% less likely to develop heart disease over a period of 5 to 25 years.

Cherry (2023) also added that researchers have found that maintaining a positive attitude may be associated with a longer lifespan. Another study also found that people with a positive outlook were more likely to make healthy lifestyle choices like exercising and eating a healthy diet.

I'd say that positive thinking is a superpower. It helps you take action. You can cope with challenges better. You can think more creatively and solve problems more effectively.

Positive thinking can also improve your relationships with others. People will enjoy your company more because a positive mood is contagious. You need to cultivate this superpower.

Here's a bonus, you deserve one: According to a study from the University of Kansas, even a forced smile can reduce heart rate and blood pressure in stressful situations. So even if you're feeling angry or frustrated, taking a few minutes to watch something funny, even if you don't feel like it, could help you calm down.

A smile on you looks great. Just saying though.

STRENGTHS-BASED APPROACH

Xie (2013) shared that people with mental illnesses often view themselves in a negative light due to a combination of factors. The medical model of mental illness, which emphasizes pathology, can reinforce feelings of shame and failure, leading to low self-esteem.

However, a strength-based approach, which focuses on each person's unique strengths and abilities, may be a more effective way to support people with mental illness and help them recover.

The strength-based approach views the individual as the one who takes actions and drives their own change. It emphasizes the individual's unique resources and abilities, rather than their deficits or diagnoses.

This approach recognizes that how a person interprets their thoughts and emotions is an important factor in their well-being. It's also based on the idea that people are inherently capable of growth and positive changes.

The approach also considers the individual's environment, identifying any social, personal, or cultural factors that may be holding them back. By empowering the individual and helping them draw on their strengths, this approach aims to foster positive change and personal growth.

Marschall (2024) stated that in strength-based therapy, the goal is to help the individual see themselves in a positive light and develop a resilient, resourceful mindset. This can be especially useful when facing adversity, as it allows the individual to draw on their own strengths and capabilities to navigate challenges.

In other words, it fosters a "can-do" rather than "can't-do" mentality. Do you think this kind of mindset is helpful when dealing with difficult circumstances?

The strength-based approach is a therapeutic approach that you can't do yourself. You'll need a therapist who is acquainted with the approach. The therapist will also check your suitability for the therapy before starting.

However, if you believe that the approach will be beneficial to you, get in touch with a therapist who knows about it and work on something together.

FINDING MEANING AND PURPOSE

Another way to view positive psychology is to see it as a branch of psychology that focuses on what makes life meaningful and how people can thrive. Thus, the concept of finding meaning and purpose is still within the ambit of positive psychology.

I've learned that life can be much more beautiful and meaningful than what we've thought it to be. Daily routines, rituals, just living for the paycheck, or just getting by has a way of making us numb to the purpose of living. Thus, we lose touch with the essence of our existence just trying to stay alive.

People who don't have a positive attitude towards life don't see any higher reason for it other than just filling the space. They don't think that there's anything to live or even fight for.

Have you seen someone who wakes up every morning all excited about what the day brings to them? For someone like that, there's something within them that drives them to step out of their bed and get their day started already. They're living for something.

In addition to everything you've learned up to this point, you have to start believing that there's more to your life than what you've discovered. There's more to you than being a child, a parent, a friend, or a colleague. There's more to your life than being a manager or an employee. Your life can't just be defined by those titles or what you earn.

You were made for a higher purpose. That drive within you that makes you think of doing something different in your community or for someone, is an indication that you have more to do with your life than just getting by. Do you agree with me?

Whether you're fighting for racial justice, helping children to learn to read, creating inspiring art, or volunteering your time and resources during a crisis, it's important to find ways to bring your unique strengths to the table and use them for good.

In doing so, you can not only contribute to the world around you, but also find more fulfillment in your own life.

Science suggests that having a sense of purpose is associated with a variety of benefits, including better physical and mental health, increased longevity, and even increased earning potential.

Finding your purpose can give you a deep sense of fulfillment and meaning in life, knowing that you're making a positive impact on the world with your unique talents and skills.

Even if it's just one person you're using your skills and resources to help, it's still something. It will give you a sense of direction and motivation, as you work toward something greater than yourself.

To find meaning in life, you have to start by identifying something you care about. Once you have a general sense of what matters to you and what skills you bring to the table, think of ways to apply your skills and abilities in that direction.

Also, try imagining the best possible version of yourself in the next couple of years. It can serve as a motivating force to get going.

Just remember, your purpose doesn't have to be something grand. It's okay if you're not seen all over social media or interviewed on major TV stations. What matters is that you're making at least one person happy. To that person, you're a hero. So your purpose can be a series of small, meaningful steps in the right direction.

NURTURING POSITIVE CONNECTIONS

None of us can do life alone. But since we have to, it must be with the right people. Positive, healthy relationships are nurtured in a safe environment. Nothing healthy grows in a toxic environment. It'll be choked!

Social connections are an essential part of human life, and healthy relationships are important to our emotional and mental well-being. Whether with family, friends, romantic partners, or colleagues, strong relationships can provide us with a sense of belonging, mutual support, and fulfillment.

But then, to build and nurture positive connections requires effort, patience, and the ability to communicate effectively.

Have you tried building a relationship and it didn't work? Can you share what happened?

_____

_____

_____

_____

Well, you're better equipped to try again, right? That's the spirit!

Positive relationships don't just benefit you alone, it can extend to the people around you as well. The ripple effect of your positivity and good relationships can extend to your team, customer, and your community.

In addition to everything you've learned, being your authentic self is one of the building blocks to forming real, meaningful relationships. Take off the mask and stop the charades.

I know it requires a level of courage to let others see the real you, but being vulnerable allows you to build deeper bonds with others based on shared interests and experiences. Positive connections that leads to trust, understanding, and happiness thrive in positive environments.

THE ROLE OF POSITIVE PSYCHOLOGY IN OVERCOMING ADVERSITY AND BUILDING RESILIENCE

In the previous chapter, I shared how EQ and resilience are linked and how they make people thrive in the face of adversity. Let's build on that because it's connected.

Positive psychology encourages an optimistic outlook and a growth mindset, same as EQ. These two tools—a positive outlook and a growth mindset—are powerful tools for building resilience.

An optimistic mindset is one in which you see setbacks as temporary challenges, rather than permanent failures. It's the belief that you can improve yourself and your circumstances with effort and perseverance.

When you also have a positive self-image, you believe in your abilities and potential for growth. This can help you become more resilient in the face of adversity. You are more likely to believe you can overcome challenges, learn from mistakes, and find new ways to succeed. These positive beliefs fuel the optimism and perseverance that enable resilience.

Do you want to know how else positive psychology builds resilience? Having a clear sense of meaning and purposeful living! That's why I spoke about meaningful living before this.

People who have a clear sense of meaning and live purposefully are resilient. They have goals, values, or a sense of mission that gives them a sense of purpose even in challenging times.

This purpose provides a strong foundation to fall back on when life is difficult. They improvise or invent new ways to forge ahead in the face of adversity. They have inner motivation to persevere hardship and find strength to keep moving forward.

CREATING A POSITIVE LIFE VISION

Living a meaningful life also entails having a vision for living. Setting a clear vision for your life can have powerful benefits. Having a defined vision can give you a sense of purpose and direction.

It can help you to see opportunities and opportunities that you might otherwise miss. While it may sometimes feel difficult to set and achieve goals, a positive mindset can help you make progress.

To create a positive vision, let's take off from the things I shared with you under the *Finding Meaning and Purpose* section. Remember you have to:

- Identify the things that matter to you.
- Identify your skills and resources—in this context your strength.
- Envision your best life possible.

These create something to work with when creating a life vision. You know, vision is the power to imagine the future and see possibilities that may come to be. It gives direction and motivation needed to turn your goals and purpose into reality. That's what a visionary life entails.

Let's make it more practical:

1. Write your vision down. Your journal can come in handy here.
2. Set a time for your vision.
3. Define your goal
4. Make plans on how to achieve your goal. Break your plans into small chunks of activities to make it easier for you to track.

5. Celebrate each milestone.

Case Study

Adams was wrongfully convicted of a crime he didn't commit and spent 10 years in prison. While in prison, he became determined to learn the law and understand the case that landed him there.

With his self-taught legal knowledge, he was able to find a flaw in his defense and get his conviction overturned. After gaining his freedom, he became an attorney and committed himself to helping others in similar situations.

When you read Adams' story, what themes stood out boldly to you?

_____

_____

_____

_____

WORKBOOK 4

1. Write a list of 5 things you're grateful for.

1. _____

2. _____

3. _____

4. _____

5. _____

2. Identify one thing you're passionate about.

1. Identify the skills you need to make that thing happen.
2. Mention three ways you can apply your skills to that passion and make some impact, no matter how little.

TAKEAWAY 4

- Positive emotions don't grow like negativity, just as normal plants don't grow like weeds. They require intentional effort starting with clearing out negativity. Then you sow the seeds of positive emotions and you begin to nurture them till they have strong roots in your mind.
- If what you desire is to have a great life, then start thinking of greatness instead of impossibilities, failure, and disappointment. Positive thinking is so powerful that it can shape your life to become what you constantly think it to be.

Positive psychology and everything it entails is just what we need to live a purposeful life filled with happiness and satisfaction.

It might interest you to know that there's a therapeutic side of things to recreating your perspective of life and shifting from a negative wiring to a more positive view. That will be the focus of the next chapter.

CHAPTER "GOOD WILL"

Helping others without expectation of anything in return has been proven to lead to increased happiness and satisfaction in life.

I would love to give you the chance to experience that same feeling during your reading or listening experience today...

All it takes is a few moments of your time to answer one simple question:

<u>Would you make a difference in the life of someone you've never met—without spending any money or seeking recognition for your good will?</u>

If so, I have a small request for you.

If you've found value in your reading or listening experience today, I humbly ask that you take a brief moment right now to leave an honest review of this book. It won't cost you anything but 30 seconds of your time— just a few seconds to share your thoughts with others.

Your voice can go a long way in helping someone else find the same inspiration and knowledge that you have.

Are you familiar with leaving a review for an Audible, Kindle, or e-reader book? If so, it's simple:

If you're on **Audible**: just hit the three dots in the top right of your device, click rate & review, then leave a few sentences about the book along with your star rating.

If you're reading on **Kindle** or an e-reader, simply scroll to the last page of the book and swipe up—the review should prompt from there.

If you're on a **Paperback** or any other physical format of this book, you can find the book page on Amazon (or wherever you bought this) and leave your review right there.

CBT TECHNIQUES FOR TRANSFORMATION

The happiness of your life depends upon the quality of your thoughts.

— MARCUS AURELIUS

In the last four chapters we dwelt more on the cyclical connection between your thoughts and emotions. We've seen how one has an effect on the other. But there's another aspect of that activity we've not elaborately discussed. It's your actions—behavioral pattern.

Thoughts produce behaviors. Your behavioral pattern is a product of your thought pattern. You can't expect someone who thinks negatively to behave otherwise. It'll be contradictory. If we include behavior into that cyclical pattern, we'll have thoughts leading to emotions and emotions producing behaviors.

But then it could also be your behavior leading to your thoughts and thoughts producing your emotions. It's cyclical. The objective of this chapter is to take you a step further in your transformational journey by magnifying the effects of thoughts on behavior, and vice-versa. I'll also introduce you to a proven therapeutic option that can reprogramme the flow of negativity in both spheres.

PRINCIPLES AND APPLICATIONS OF COGNITIVE BEHAVIORAL THERAPY (CBT)

CBT is a therapy technique that helps people recognize and challenge negative thoughts and behaviors that may be causing them distress. CBT aims to help people understand and change unhelpful patterns of thinking and behaving that can lead to mental health problems.

CBT works by identifying and correcting faulty thinking patterns that can lead to negative thoughts and behaviors. By breaking these cognitive errors, or unhelpful ways of thinking, and reframing them in a more rational and positive way, CBT can help improve mental health and well-being.

I like the fact that CBT isn't rigid. It's flexible and adaptable to suit each person's dynamic needs. However, there are some common underlying principles that are relevant to everyone.

There are some principles of CBT which I'll take you through in a moment.

Principle #1

CBT is an approach that evolves as patients learn and change. The therapist continually assesses the patient's problems and understands their thoughts and feelings in a cognitive way. This personalized approach helps patients understand themselves better.

Principle #2

CBT thrives on the relationship between the therapist and patient. A strong therapeutic connection between therapist and patient is important to the effectiveness of CBT.

Principle #3

CBT isn't just about telling the patient what to do or think, instead, the therapist and patient work together to identify and understand the patient's thought patterns and behaviors.

Principle #4

CBT is goal-driven. The therapist works with the patient to define specific goals for the patient to achieve to solve the patient's specific problem. So CBT is also personalized, problem-focused.

Principle #5

CBT focuses on the present moment, rather than delving into a patient's past. Although understanding the origin of the patient's thoughts, feelings, and behaviors is important, the primary goal is to help the patient make positive changes in the moment.

Principle #6

CBT is designed to be time-efficient, so that the patient can learn to manage their own mental health over the long term.

Thus the therapist's role is to educate the patient on CBT techniques and help them learn how to apply these techniques in their daily life.

In addition, CBT also helps patients learn to anticipate and prevent setbacks, so they can stay on track in the future.

What do you think about this therapeutic option? Is it something you'd like to try out?

COGNITIVE RESTRUCTURING

Cognitive restructuring is one of the key components of CBT. It includes a set of tools that can help you recognize and change negative thought patterns. These tools will help you identify negative distortions in your thoughts and replace them with something more realistic and helpful.

So, let's say that someone has been thinking loudly in their head, "I fail at everything." Through cognitive restructuring, the thought can be slowly replaced with, "I may have had some failures, but I've also had successes. I'm getting better at this."

Sounds realistic, right? The goal of these tools isn't to make people think positively, rather to have more balanced and realistic thoughts.

Cognitive restructuring isn't a rigid, stereotypical process that everyone follows in the same way. Instead, a person's specific situations and needs are taken into account. You can learn it and apply it on your own, but working with a trained therapist can make the process more effective.

Nevertheless, let's see what you can do for yourself.

One of the tools of cognitive restructuring is self-monitoring. This tool entails an attempt to recognize and identify the unproductive thought patterns that cause negative emotions. This is similar to what we discuss under self-awareness. It's a tool that can help you start changing the way you think first by recognizing what you've been thinking.

It will also be useful to recognize situations in which these patterns tend to occur. With this information, you can plan ahead and prepare yourself to respond in different ways.

There's also something called "Socratic questioning." It involves asking yourself questions to challenge your negative assumptions and automatic thoughts. The idea is to identify the biases in your thinking, rather than trying to defend or justify them.

You can start out with questions like:

- Is this thought an emotional reaction, or is it based on logic and evidence?
- What facts support this thought?
- What evidence contradicts this thought?
- Is there a way to test this thought?

Questioning is a powerful way of rebelling against something. Keep those questions going.

Another tool in cognitive restructuring is to think of the cost of your negative distortion. Think of the benefits and disadvantages of holding on to that thought pattern. This may involve comparing the positive aspects of maintaining a thought with the negative aspects of maintaining it. If you're able to find its cost, you'll be able to weigh your options and make better decisions.

BEHAVIORAL ACTIVATION

Villines (2021) describes behavioral activation as an approach to improving mental health that involves taking action in the real world. The idea is that our behaviors can influence our emotions, and so we can feel better by doing things that make us feel good.

This approach can also be thought of as a CBT technique, but it can stand on its own.

Depression has been the most studied mental health issue in line with this approach. This is because people with depression often have low motivation to do things that used to bring them joy.

Therefore, behavioral activation is one way to re-engage with activities and experiences that were previously rewarding. Have you seen any depressed persons before or you've been there before?

Something you'll notice about them is the decrease in the amount of time they spend on activities that used to be meaningful to them. This can make symptoms worse, especially if they were a way to stay connected to others or feel good about themselves.

The goal of behavioral activation, therefore, is to encourage people to engage more antidepressant behaviors. This can include socializing with friends or pursuing hobbies they used to enjoy.

You can break the cycle of depression by taking action, even if you don't feel like it at first. Behavioral activation encourages you to act even if you're not currently interested in them. It has been proven to be an effective treatment for depression in a number of studies.

When you start acting, that's just the first step. Becoming aware of how much activity you're currently engaging in is important. It'll help you see the patterns and connections between your level of activities and your mood.

Another step in this approach is to identify your values and goals. When you determine what is truly important to you, it'll help you develop meaningful goals to work towards. This will help you create a sense of purpose and give you the right motivation for the activities.

Now, the activities you should start with should be simple, but they should be able to give you pleasure and a sense of fulfillment. It could be something like going for a walk, reading a book, washing the dishes.

It could also help to write down these activities so that as you complete them you tick them off. That act alone gives you a sense of fulfillment. Try it.

EXPOSURE THERAPY

Do you know that there are people who are leaving in fear due to negative thinking patterns?

Those distorted thought patterns can make people afraid and timid in certain cases. And in extreme cases, it leads to what's called phobia. You wonder what could make someone afraid of water or height. It's rooted in distorted thinking.

But this is not to judge them. Their distorted thinking could be a product of things that aren't their fault. For some, it could be something rooted in their childhood. But the goal here isn't to dig into the past, we're focusing on what can be done in the present moment.

Talking of the present moment, there's a therapeutic option that can ease the elimination of fear. It's called exposure therapy. This technique will help you face your fears in a safe and controlled way.

What do we do when we're afraid of something? Avoid it, right? Avoidance is often the natural response, but it does no good in the long run. Avoiding things that scare us may provide short-term relief, but it can worsen our fear over time.

It can also limit our ability to enjoy activities and live a fulfilling life. With exposure therapy, you can break this cycle and live without being limited by your fear. You'll learn to tolerate fear without negative consequences.

In exposure therapy, you'll also learn that the thoughts you have when you're afraid aren't realistic. Through the process of gradual exposure, you'll learn to feel more comfortable in situations that used to cause fear.

So, this therapy is based on the idea that we learn through experience and that we can change our beliefs based on new evidence.

There are different types of exposure therapy with the same goal. The type you go for with your therapist is dependent on the situation you want to deal with. But the approach is usually almost the same.

First, your therapist might have you simply talk about what you're afraid of, let's say flying. Then at the next session, you might be asked to watch videos of planes taking off and landing.

After that, you might be asked to watch the video from the perspective of a passenger inside the plane. And then gradually, the therapist would take you to a plane in real life. First you might just be asked to stand next to a plane, then you go inside and sit in the cabin. Then you'll remain seated to take a short flight.

This continues until that fear is decimated and dealt with eventually. So, exposure therapy is usually done best with a support system, like a professional and it's gradual.

MINDFULNESS-BASED COGNITIVE THERAPY

Mindfulness-based cognitive therapy (MBCT) was designed to help people who have had multiple episodes of depression. It combines ideas from mindfulness meditation with CBT.

The goal is to teach people how to be more aware of the present moment, so that they can reduce depressive thinking and negative moods.

MBCT teaches people how to approach their thoughts and feelings from a place of curiosity and acceptance. People are encouraged to notice their negative or upsetting thoughts and feelings without getting caught up in them or trying to change them.

They learn to observe their own thoughts without judgment. This can help them break free from patterns of destructive thinking. So, being closely related to CBT, it MBCT combines elements of CBT with mindfulness meditation to help people overcome negative thinking patterns.

The cognitive therapy techniques help them recognize and question negative patterns. Mindfulness on the other hand helps people to replace the negative thoughts with more positive ones.

The combination of these two approaches is thought to help people with depression change their thought patterns in a more lasting way

MBCT is designed to teach people how to break the thought patterns that can lead to depression. One study showed that MBCT was effective at preventing depression relapse as taking medication (Schimelpfening, 2024).

PROBLEM-SOLVING SKILLS

Problem-solving skills is another CBT-driven tool that helps people develop the skills they need to identify, evaluate, and solve problems. It teaches people to break down big problems into smaller, more manageable steps. This therapy is thought to reduce stress and improve physical and mental health.

If you've learned problem-solving skills during a therapy session, you're more likely to be able to cope with stressors and life changes without relapses. The key is to practice these skills on an ongoing basis, not just during therapy sessions.

So, the first step will be to identify the problem. Learn how to recognize when there's a problem that needs to be solved. For instance if you have trouble falling asleep at night. That's the problem that needs solving.

Afterwards, think of some possible solutions. It could be going to bed earlier, having a warm bath before bedtime, reading a book instead of using screens, or using relaxation techniques.

Once you've come up with possible solutions, weigh each solution by considering their advantages and disadvantages. After you've done that, go ahead to choose the solution with greater advantage and which suits your needs best.

And of course, you have to move on to implementation. But that shouldn't mark the end of your problem solving. You have to assess the outcome of the solution you chose if it gives you the result you desire.

RELAXATION TECHNIQUES

Negative thoughts have a way of stressing you out. When you worry a lot, ruminate, or dwell on your past mistakes, it leads to stress. Stress is neither good for your mental health nor your physical health. You could become emotionally unstable and react with negative emotions. This surely has some ripple effects.

But since we've been talking about transformation, there's yet another technique you could practice to calm yourself when you're feeling anxious and stressed. Relaxation techniques can help you reduce tension and promote feelings of relaxation in your body.

While practicing relaxation techniques, you're usually advised to focus on these things – your breath, certain image or sound, and senses. One of the relaxation techniques you can practice for breath is breathing exercise.

Start by getting into a comfortable seated position with your spine straight. Then place one hand on your stomach. Next, breathe in through your nose and pay attention to your stomach expanding.

Afterwards, breathe out through your mouth and pay attention to your stomach relax. Repeat this exercise until you feel calm.

Another great exercise in relaxation techniques pertains to images. It's primarily about focusing on a soothing image to achieve calmness. So, you can start by getting into a relaxed position, sitting or lying down. Close your eyes and begin to breathe slowly and deeply in such a way that you're conscious of it.

Now, imagine that soothing image while your eyes are still closed. Focus your senses on the image—smell, sound, beauty, etc. What you'll notice is that you'll be carried away into the context you've created in your mind. You'll almost be unaware of what's happening around you. The goal is to achieve calm.

STRATEGIES FOR SUSTAINABLE CHANGE

I desire nothing else other than to see you experience transformation. It's just a matter of time before you begin to get the results you desire. This will happen as you consistently apply the techniques and information I've shared with you till this point.

Now, when the changes begin to take place, try as much as you can not to stop doing the things that produced those changes. To experience sustainable change, you have to keep at your exercises and routines until they become a part of you. Until they become things you can do almost subconsciously.

You won't want to relapse to negative expressions after taking steps into the positivity zone. Now, I'd like to state here that as you begin to apply the things you've learned so far, you'll likely experience setbacks. What should be your attitude towards them? Resilience.

Likewise to experience sustainable transformation, you have to be resilient. You shouldn't throw in the towel when the results aren't coming in as quick as you expect. You shouldn't recline into your former pattern of thinking and behavior because something unpleasant made you feel bad. You should fight back to stay in the positive zone.

Another strategy is to stay committed and active in your support community. Don't lose touch with your support community. Community is a powerful place where change takes place. It's also a great place to sustain the change. So, just as you're changing, you can also help others experience change. And while you're doing that, you'll be encouraged to stay on track since it's no more about you alone.

Something else you can do is to keep revisiting your vision and reviewing your goals. Do you remember that you had a vision of the best possible version of yourself in years to come? That's the vision that got you started on the path of transformation. Until you arrive there, don't stop making progress. No matter the amount of success you achieve, keep going.

Then in order to keep that vision alive, always review your goals and plans as you move past a phase of the transformational experience.

One last strategy I'll share is to be a learner. Don't stop learning. Learning is one of the powerful ways I know that sustains change. The moment you stop learning, someone said you start dying. But in this context, you might become stagnant and reduce in value.

Case Study

Emily was a young professional who struggled with severe anxiety. It didn't start as something disturbing. However, it grew till it began to affect her productivity at work. Her relationships also suffered for it.

Her anxiety grew as illogical thoughts created crippling fear and worry in her, therefore making it difficult to concentrate at anything. Emily became paranoid. She became so sensitive that she perceived threats in a chit-chat.

Eventually, she had to take a break from work when it was becoming obvious she might lose on two ends if she didn't seek help.

Emily didn't start out as a paranoid young woman. She must have had some disturbing experiences that made way for the negativity that took over her mind. It's her recognition of a need for help that interests me the most.

The moment you realize that you need some help to get your life back on track, you're halfway into the transformation experience.

WORKBOOK 5

1. Identify 2 dominant negative thoughts you've spent time ruminating on severally.

   1. Are those thoughts based on emotional reaction or logic and evidence?
   2. What facts support those thoughts?

2. Define your vision for living.

   1. State a specific, time-bound (short-term) goal that resonates with your vision.
   2. Create plans that will enable you to fulfill the goal.
   3. Assess your progress and then go again.

TAKEAWAY 5

- The moment you realize that your thoughts are suggestions, not unbreakable laws, that's when you start restructuring your behavioral pattern.
- Questioning your thoughts is a powerful way of stripping negative thoughts of their influence on your actions.
- Transformation requires effort. Sustaining it takes more, however, the approach to both are

similar. Through resilience, practice, and a growth mindset, transformation can become permanent.

The second part of this book has taken us through a transformative route to attaining peace and total well-being. This chapter which marks the end of the second phase not only showed ways to be transformed mentally and physically, but also how to sustain it.

Now, everything is set for you to attain peace and experience healing in relationships. That's the climax of this book. Take a breather. Reflect. Before you embark on the final lap. I'll be waiting for you on the other side.

PART III

FINDING PEACE

We're back to where we began: a peaceful mind, not a quiet mind.

Some time ago, a nature photographer captured a bird sitting calmly on the branch of a dancing tree. From the picture, it's easy to tell that a heavy rain was beating hard on the tree. Yet, the bird sat calmly on that tree.

Now, I'd say that's a clear depiction of peace.

In this part, the focus will be on how to foster inner peace and maintain it despite the noise around. Most times, you don't have the power to shut down the noise, but what you can do is to ensure the noise doesn't upset you.

This will lead us to having peace in your past and present relationships as well. This part is the crowning piece of your transformational journey.

6

FOSTERING INNER PEACE

There is peace even in the storm.

— VINCENT VAN GOGH

Negative thoughts are disruptive. They can be really unsettling. When you allow them to stay longer than welcome, they influence your emotions and behavior. Negative thoughts could also create fear in your heart and make you anxious.

As these actions and reactions are taking place within you, it may lead to a restless mind. Now, it's rare to think straight when your mind loses its peace. Your choices in that context cannot be trusted to be credible.

But then, do you know that it's possible to experience peace despite those activities within you?

Here's how:

THE PARALYSIS OF ANALYSIS

Have you ever been in a situation where you had to make a quick decision but couldn't because you spent so much time thinking about your options?

For example, you had five days to accept an offer. A great opportunity that could transform your financial status. But just while you're excited about the offer, you started analyzing the pros and cons of the offer so much that you missed the deadline date.

You thought about all possible options. At some point, you began to fear that things might not go as the offer painted it. You became anxious and agitated while trying to analyze every possible outcome. Eventually, you missed the offer.

If you do this for every opportunity you get or choice you have to make, it won't be long before you'll be stuck, unable to make progress in life. Do you know why? You will never make any decision because you would have overthought the choice so much that you'll be afraid of making any decision. So, you keep procrastinating because you don't want to make the wrong decision.

But logically, you're actually making a decision—a decision not to decide—that is the worst kind of decision. That's what analysis paralysis is about. You thought about your choices so much that you're unable to take any action because you're afraid of making the wrong move.

Clarke (2022) describes analysis paralysis as being in an overly confused state when you're about to take action on a situation or you want to make a decision. I understand that you have to think through your decisions and weigh all options. That's necessary. But overthinking the pros and cons can cloud your ability to make decisions.

Paralysis, medically, is a state of immobility or inactivity. That's what happens when you overthink issues and don't eventually take any action. You get stuck.

It might seem that the more you think about an issue, the more clear your decisions will be. But haven't you realized that the more you think about the matter, the more difficult it gets? The longer you stay in the state of indecision, the harder it becomes to make a choice.

This leads to fear and anxiety and that can lead to another round of overthinking based on your feelings.

That's one strong web you don't want to get caught in. It robs of peace and, if not careful, sanity.

You'll also experience stress-related symptoms, like loss of sleep, loss of focus, increased heart rate, fatigue, anxiety, ruminating thoughts, etc.

If you're experiencing this, you risk being isolated and left behind. Indecision makes people miss out on opportunities and experiences. It can also lead to an inferiority complex because you'll doubt your ability to make good decisions.

But then, this doesn't happen with all kinds of decisions, just primarily life-shaping choices, like career, marriage or relationships, or jobs. The basis of your fears could be genuine.

It could be due to some past experiences, so you're afraid of making the same mistake. It could even be other people's experiences that's causing your indecision.

But the question is, would you rather stay stuck in the past or let other people's experiences affect your progress?

It's safe to stay indoors while it's raining, right? But you can also miss out on the joy and fun of dancing in the rain.

Analysis paralysis isn't a life sentence, you can be healed and get your life advancing again. But it begins with making this first decision: I WANT TO ADVANCE.

This singular decision will propel every other thing you need to do. But if you make that first decision, it means that the same energy you put into overthinking will be rechanneled to productive thinking.

One of the things that leads to overthinking is that you overly forecast into the future. The question is, do any of us have control over the future? Do all our plans for the future always turn out exactly the way we planned them?

I doubt if the answers will be affirmative. This is where I get to tell you that mindfulness practice will come in handy here again. Be rooted in the moment. Don't worry about tomorrow. Make your decisions based on the facts and statistics you have at hand, not the ones you're creating in your head.

Only perfectionists want everything to go as they plan it. Once they notice any crack in their plan, they start the thinking process again. The issue with that is, it takes more time, leads to another round of anxiety, and more thinking.

So, instead of being mindful of the perfect outcome, focus more on your progress. That's more important. Take small steps forward. Stop at any point if you need to reconsider your options or your plan. You have the right and choice to do this in a relationship, career, or any other thing.

Why don't you cut yourself some slack and allow yourself to make mistake? Life is a risk. None of us has it figured out. Do you know why? Change is constant. So, things can change when we least expect it. Be flexible.

Don't beat yourself if you're wrong with the decision. Even if it does, it won't be so bad that you'll have to lose so much. Rather, it will be a leverage to lead you to your next most important opportunity. You're capable of doing the right thing and making the right decisions. If you hear otherwise, it's a lie!

Then I'd say, simply ask. Wherever you need clarity, just ask instead of trying to figure it out yourself. It makes it easier.

Case Study

As a young man in the professional space, Lester knew his strengths and weaknesses. And he knew that no matter what decision he made, he could succeed at it. But that knowledge had left him stagnating for 15 years.

He's always overwhelmed with the endless possibilities that he couldn't nail down what he wanted to do with his life. He knew it wasn't a matter of intelligence or ability. According to him, it's more like a scene from The Notebook: It's like Allie, asking, "What do you want?" His answer is always, "I don't know!"

PRIORITIZE SELF-VALIDATION

It's natural to seek validation. You stepped out in a new cloth. When people say nice things about it, you blush. It makes you happy. You took time to work on a project, it's natural to expect some praise for the work or the effort you invested.

It's not out of place to expect it. It's a good way to stay motivated to forge ahead. However, when your expectations become excessive, it leads to such unhealthy behaviors like people-pleasing. So you try to win people's approval by all means. You might change who you are, compromise on your values, or what you do to please others.

It's when you excessively seek people's validation that you get stressed. When people don't give you the right amount of validation, you might start to think that there's something wrong with what you did or said.

With the hype on social media platforms, many people now base their worth on the likes and comments they get on each of their posts. They go to the extent of checking their phones every moment to see how much feedback they've gotten. When they don't get enough or any, they feel critical and negative.

This makes you lose your peace because you'll start thinking of different things. That's when you'll remember flimsy thingslike:

"their body language said it all,"

"did you notice nobody smiled?"

"no one paid attention, they all focused on him,"

"could it be that..."

"What if..."

These are all shades of negative thoughts. If this lingers, depression is looming just by the corner. Low self-esteem is already setting up a seat in your mind. External validations are good, but if we don't get them, we shouldn't become self-critical to the point of losing sight of the goodness in us.

It's true that you're not perfect, but you're not all bad. If you've made some effort to say something or do something nice, it means that you're actually worth something. Maybe others are just too busy to see it. But that's not what matters most.

What matters most is what you think of yourself. Internal validation is really essential if you want to enjoy inner peace. Did you also know that you won't give room for growth if you keep depending on people's comments to determine your worth?

Internal validation is a great way to ensure you're perpetually growing. At least, your mind will be clear enough to embrace positive criticisms and grow where necessary. Unlike when your mind is veiled with clouds of self-doubt, self-criticism, and the likes.

To validate yourself, define "WHO" you are" and "WHY" you do what you do. Your "who" talks about your identity while your "why" points to your purpose. If you don't answer these questions, people will tell you who they think you should be and what they think you should be doing.

Those two questions create a base for everything you do. Any external validation that doesn't align with your who and why isn't relevant to you.

Don't ever think low or talk low of yourself. Never! You're your best cheerleader and brand manager. Every other person might be doing it for you for some profits, but you. You're doing it for yourself because you believe in YOU.

Even when you aren't doing too well, what you say to yourself matters. Appreciate yourself for the effort and resources you put into doing something. It's a lot! The result might not be great, celebrate the process.

And when you have little wins, celebrate them too! Don't be too timid to tell yourself, "You did well." "Thank you!" Before anyone else starts telling you, do it yourself.

Another great fact you should know about people is that they're insatiable and their preferences always. Don't rely too much on them. Social media, especially, is a place where people say anything they like without restriction. Don't build your life on all you read there.

SHUTTING OUT BIASED SOCIETAL VIEWS

The loudest societal views today are in the media—print and online. The media thinks they own a right to your life, so they can say just about anything. There are different motives behind what people say in the media.

Some are propaganda while some are with the intention to gain some popularity. Therefore, many of those posts and comments are with some bias and sentiments. There's always a motive behind them. They actually don't mind what their agenda does to their target.

Just imagine someone doing a video to claim that your newborn baby doesn't have your look or your spouse', but another person you're close to. As a result, there has been foul play somewhere. What effrontery!

That's the type of audacity you get from society. There's a lot of shaming, racism, bullying, deception, gender-bias, etc., out there—physical and online. Those things are damaging. If every time you scroll through different timelines, all you get are negative vibes, then it's time to shut down.

I understand that you might want to stay abreast of the latest info and trends, that's good. However, if you're doing that at the expense of your mental health, you should prioritize your health. Trends don't end.

Take a break from social media. Or if your work requires that you go there once and again, make yourself less visible there. Do whatever your work demands that you do. Turn off notifications.

Also, don't bother reading every headline or story that jumps at you when you're trying to do your work there. Don't be tempted to give them a moment of your time.

If your work doesn't demand you stay online, then take a break.

Although you can turn off social media, you can't do the same for other aspects of society. So what do you do?

Have an open mind to diversity. Don't be rigid in your opinion about things and people. Be open to meeting people from different backgrounds, experiences, and culture. It's a good way to shut down biases.

Also, don't shut out marginalized voices. Their perspectives of life count as well. This means that you shouldn't be rigid. You know, your personal bias could make you judgmental and even have wrong perspectives about people.

What's the effect of that? You'll experience setbacks in relationships with your society. You can't live in isolation, you know? So, question your assumptions and biases. You don't have to rush things. Just take it a step at a time.

OVERCOMING PERFECTIONISM

Are you aware that excellence isn't the same as perfectionism? Oh, I'm so big on excellence. But perfectionism? Can't say the same for it.

Excellence and perfectionism might look the same on the surface, but their distinctive difference is in their core meanings. Excellence is a continuous commitment to being the best you can be. Perfectionism, on the other hand, is striving to be flawless.

Both concepts do not give room for flaws, however, it's the attitudes to flaws that makes them different. For someone striving to be the best at something, they recognize the place of failing forward. That is, while trying to be the best, they can make some mistakes. However, instead of being self-critical. They rise up. Assess what went wrong and try again.

It's different with perfectionism. A perfectionist's attitude to flaws is sometimes unforgiven. They can beat themselves hard for any slight mistake. Perfectionism can be toxic and can lead to low self-esteem, anxiety, and depression. Even though its intentions are good, the means are not.

Perfectionism might look like excellence, but it's not. Excellence is growth-driven. Excellence is about setting realistic goals. It gives you room to embrace your imperfections, while perfectionism rejects them.

Nothing is more peaceful than knowing that you're not under pressure to prove anything to anyone. You're more comfortable to keep growing at your pace, not complacent. You're putting in the time to grow when you should. And you keep getting better. Even if perfectionism also wants growth, the pressure is always high.

Embrace excellence. You're not competing against anyone, but yourself. Your motivation for growth shouldn't be anyone else but you. This means that you have a blueprint of your visions and goals. And what you desire to become. So, you keep striving to arrive there.

And just as I stated in self-validation, be your biggest cheerleader. Celebrate your wins. Encourage yourself to rise again when you falter at something. Always have these in your vocabulary: "I'll try again" and "I'm not done, yet. It can be better."

I'd also like to include, don't deprive yourself of rest. Rest allows your body and mind to recuperate and get ready to go again. If you don't, you won't have a vessel to get you to your goals.

WHAT'S YOUR HAPPINESS BASED ON?

What do you mean when you say, "I'm happy today"? What made you happy? I'm just curious to know. Do you know why?

We all desire happiness. It's that sense of satisfaction and fulfillment. However, I'm aware that what happiness means for each of us differs. And the things we seek happiness in differ as well.

But what I also know is that our definition of happiness also impacts our actions, pursuits, and commitments. For instance, someone who finds happiness in eating pizza, will do everything necessary to get pizza daily. This could also include when they don't have the financial capacity for it. They'll do anything just to be happy.

The happiness described in the example above is from immediate gratification. For another person, it could be completing a set of tasks or winning a trophy. The diverse description of happiness makes happiness a subjective emotional state.

One thing that's common with happiness for everyone is that it comes with a sense of satisfaction with any area of our lives. So, when you're looking out for signs of happiness, you'll see them in how someone is willing to take on life as it comes. You'll also see it in someone whose relationship is positive and healthy. Feeling satisfied and accomplished in life is a sign that comes with living a happy life. Expressing gratitude is a sign that one is happy.

Happiness is not necessarily what's expressed outwardly first, it starts from the mind before the outward expression. In essence, happiness is a state of the mind before it's an outward expression.

Psychologically, the types of happiness we experience comes from these three broad categories — pleasure, meaning, and engagement. Sometimes, it could be a combination of pleasure and meaning that produces that feeling or just engagement—commitment to a cause.

How do we achieve this state of the mind?

To experience happiness daily, try to start with writing out a list of things you'd like to do that day. As you set out to do them, tick each one off the list when they're completed. Such feelings of satisfaction that usually accompany that accomplishment can't be measured.

What if you don't complete those tasks? Don't feel bad. Negative thoughts could pop up. You could even blame yourself or someone else for not completing them. If you do that, it'll overshadow the feelings of satisfaction you've gotten from completing other tasks.

What you should do is to reframe your views about the tasks you couldn't finish. You're not trying to look away from what didn't work. No! You're only reframing how you see them.

To experience happiness, ensure you enjoy the moment. Happiness isn't something far away in the future. Maybe after you land your desired dream job or build your dream home or win a contract. Happiness is now. We choose to be happy now. It's a state of the mind we can choose now.

MINDFUL DETOX

I've heard of people detoxifying their body system a lot. When they do, they're trying to get rid of the junks and unhealthy stuff—toxins—from their body. They do it to cleanse their internal organs and stay healthy. How about we do the same for our minds?

Detoxifying the mind is aimed at one goal—mental health. Whenever you notice the following, you should consider a detox:

- Losing focus
- Regularly stressed
- Facing indecision
- Feeling overwhelmed with tasks
- Constant burnout
- Prone to flimsy mistakes
- Unhappy

Bodily detox takes days. Mind detox needs such a level of commitment too. So, to start. Be grateful for the season that's closing. That you're experiencing burnout or losing focus doesn't mean the season hasn't been good. It only meant you've stretched yourself through the season. And you've outlived it.

Now, acknowledge that it's time for you to refresh or move on, depending on your context. When you determine what you're in for, set an intention for it. Now, doing this will require that you take a break from everything that has pushed your mind to this extent. It could be work, relationship, or some other forms of commitment.

Take a break from your devices for that period of time too. Generally, just stay away from noise and anything that could clutter your mind.

Spend some time with yourself to evaluate what worked in the previous season. What would you like to do away with? What would you like to retain? Are there lessons you'd like to take from the previous season? Incorporate them into the new season so that you won't continue the same circle.

While doing all this, ensure you create time for rest in between. The main gist of this exercise is to stop, rest, and restart.

LETTING GO TO FIND PEACE (OTHER THINGS TO LET GO OF)

Sometimes, the key to inner peace is to let go of "what should be" and embrace "what is."

You've tried all you could to build a relationship with your colleague at work or with an aging parent, but it's not just working. It could be time to let go. When you compare yourself with others and you feel unfulfilled and intimidated, it's time to let go. Embrace your reality and be at peace with yourself.

Are you being pressured to acquire certain things or feeling inferior because you don't have them? Are you pressured that you're unmarried when all your friends are? Are you still seeking admission when all your friends have been admitted into different colleges?

Are you feeling troubled because you're still lagging when compared with others? It's time to let go and accept your present reality. This isn't the same as being complacent, accepting fate and refusing to do anything.

Letting go means giving up the unfruitful, painful chase to focus on what is present. It's about giving up on chasing things that are out of your reach and accept the present reality. Sometimes, this could be the hardest thing to do, but its reward is peace.

Come to terms with what's your reality. Your goals and aspirations are different from others'. If your pursuit doesn't align with your goals and aspirations, let it go. Why do you need a boyfriend? Why do you need the latest mobile device? Because of everyone else? Nah. Let it go. You're not everyone else.

You might eventually have those things later. That relationship you're trying to build might eventually work. But right now, embrace your goals and be committed to your daily tasks. Stop worrying about the future you can't control or some uncertain outcomes.

Oh, you don't have a boyfriend right now. Why worry? Perhaps, you don't need one now. Focus on your career, goals, or whatever you're doing that gives meaning to your existence.

You don't have the latest gadget right now? Maybe your financial capacity can't afford that yet. The connection isn't happening yet, right? Why lose your sleep over it? Perhaps, the other person needs more time or their views are different from yours. Let's try to make it work by all means.

Focus on what you have influence over today. Focus on the present moment. Every other thing—the future or an expected outcome—will take shape itself. Every good thing will come to you.

FINDING STILLNESS IN MOVEMENT

An anonymous poet once wrote: "Humans have become creatures of busyness, lively yet meaningless activities." How true that is. Mindful movement in the midst of the bustle and hustle of everyday activities ensures a healthy mental well-being.

Stillness in movement is something that has to do with your mind and your body interacting in a symphony as you engage in your daily activities. The concept of mind-body connection is essentially about the relationship between your thoughts, feelings, and body.

Your physical health can affect your mind and vice versa. In essence, when you're engaged in any physical activity, do them with awareness. You'll achieve a state of mental stillness. This stillness allows you to tune into your body, focus on the task at hand, and silence the noise in your mind.

When you're at work, take short breaks to practice some breathing techniques or simple stretches. It'll reduce stress and improve your focus. You could also use the time spent in traffic to practice mindfulness.

When you're at home doing some chores, do them mindfully by paying attention to your movements and breathing without judgment. Why's this necessary?

We've gotten so accustomed to busy lives that we now live on autopilot. Fatigue, stress, and unfulfillment will be our constant ally that way. Through mindful movement, we can reduce this.

Case Study

Alex was just a toddler when he watched the serious attack on his mom. Helpless, he stood by his mom while she gasped for life.

After the passing away of his mom, the media descended on the case with a frenzy. It left little Alex and his family in a whirlwind of public scrutiny. Legal battles ensued, further complicating the healing process.

Despite the pain and heartache he endured, Alex refused to allow his mother's death to define his life. As he became an adult, he found a path to peace and understanding.

WORKBOOK 6

1. Set aside 10-15 minutes every day to journal about your thoughts, feelings, and experiences.
2. Set aside a specific amount of time each day to disconnect from your devices.

TAKEAWAY 6

- Making a decision not to decide is the worst type of decision. It stalls you and keeps you at one spot. Resolve to advance in life is the first step to breaking that cycle of indecision.
- Excellence, not perfectionism, is what makes growth possible. Excellence is about giving your best and to keep getting better after your best output.

Finding inner peace and nurturing it is possible through intentional practices. However, it all starts with the choices you make daily. The choice to be happy in the moment. The choice to detox. The choice to take a break from external noise, etc.

When you're at peace in and with yourself, making peace with others becomes a possible stride to take. And that's what you're about to accomplish through the next chapter.

7

HEALING RELATIONSHIPS

By far the strongest poison to the human spirit is the inability to forgive oneself or another person. Forgiveness is no longer an option but a necessity for healing.

— CAROLINE MYSS

I s there anything negativity touches that it doesn't taint? Relationships are not spared. Trust and healthy communication can't thrive where negativity is. And those are the building blocks of any relationship.

Some relationships have been damaged as a result. But all is not lost yet. If any of your valuable relationships were badly affected because of a negative mindset, you can recover it.

Follow each section in this chapter to experience healing and restoration in your relationships.

IDENTIFYING AND LETTING GO OF TOXICITY

Is there anyone who has never met a toxic person all their lives? Maybe there are, but the percentage would be very low, if any. As much as we wish to keep some folks in our circle, we might not need them. Do you know why? The cost of keeping them is high.

Cost in this regard doesn't mean money per se. There are some relationships that cost emotional and/or physical investment. Some others require mental and financial investment.

Whichever one yours is, once the relationship begins to take more from you than you can give, it's unhealthy. When the relationship is also one-sided, it is toxic. Such relationships are harmful regardless of who is involved.

Healthy relationships are mutual. When both parties are committed to the well-being of each other the relationship is beneficial. But in a relationship where you are feeling undervalued, disrespected, and unsupported. That's toxic.

When you notice any of those signs in your relationship, it's time for you to reevaluate. You might have to consider letting go. By the way, relationships aren't good or bad. It's the humans in the relationship that determines its status.

If you're in a relationship with someone who treats you unfairly. I think you've endured them enough, don't you think so too? Maybe the person is always giving excuses and never taking responsibility. I think you've stood up for them long enough, right?

It's time to consider the option of letting them go. It might not be the most convenient thing to do, but it's a peaceful option. The world is full of good, loving people. You deserve one of those too. But if you don't release the toxic ones, you might not have room to receive or embrace the good ones.

If an orange doesn't taste sore in your mouth, you won't see a need to spew it. If you don't consider a relationship unhealthy, you'll keep putting up with it. Letting go starts with admitting the relationship isn't good for you.

The next thing to do is to set boundaries. Make clear about what you want and what you don't want. Let people around you know what you can tolerate and what you can't. Be firm and consistent with this. You shouldn't be sorry for setting boundaries around your life. It's a good thing to do.

Accept that you deserve good people around your life because you're good too. Accept that you deserve to be loved and valued. You'll endure just any treatment if you don't accept this truth. But you deserve more.

YOUR SUPPORT SYSTEM

An important aspect of healing in relationships is having people to lean on. When you come out of an unhealthy relationship, you might feel alone. The pain of having to let go of someone you've invested so much in could linger for a while.

But do you know the one way to go through that phase without drowning? A support system. Your support system can stand with you in such moments of need. You can feel connected and supported with your support system.

When we let go of someone, a vacuum is created in our hearts. If we don't fill it up with the right things, unhealthy things like negative thoughts can occupy that space. And you know that it can open the door to many other unhealthy things.

But having your support system around, you'll get every positive energy you need to move on. You get the encouragement, empathy, validation, and understanding you need to take the next step.

Your support system could also become a positive distraction from revisiting the past relationship. They'll give you something to get busy with and focus on depending on your bond with your support system.

Talking about support systems, they don't have to be some far away people. I'd rather that they be your family member or your friends. You could also get the right form of support from groups of people who have similar experiences and share the same belief. It could be online or physical.

To enjoy the support of any of these groups, you need to reach out. Only people who ask for help receive it. Be humble and open to ask for help. And when you do, be open and sincere.

If your support system is as good as you believe it to be, you shouldn't feel scared to be vulnerable before them. Ask questions for clarity. Don't frustrate their effort. They want to be there for you, make it easy for them.

It's supposed to be a two-way thing, right? Bear in mind that as your support system is giving you, they're investing in you. You should also be able to give back when necessary. But don't force it. Encouraging your support system with gratitude, gifts, and "check ups" is a way of giving back too.

COMMUNICATION SKILLS FOR HEALTHY RELATIONSHIPS

When two strangers meet for the first time, all they might say to each other is "hi." But when they begin to engage each other further. They are no more strangers. They'll get to know each other's interests, values, and other things.

With continuous engagement, strangers can become intimate. Don't underestimate the power of communication. On personal levels, communication determines how far a relationship will last. It's also an indicator of the health of the relationship.

On an organizational level, communication determines the productivity of an enterprise. It determines how fast things get done. But good communication skills are not things we all are born with. We all have them to different degrees. The good thing is that we can learn those skills.

Just so you know, there's more to communication than talking. But let's start with talking right. During conversations, communication has taken place when your listener understands your message and responds to it.

If none of this happened, then you've not communicated. To ensure that communication takes place, ensure your message is clear. You don't want to leave your listener wondering what exactly you're trying to say.

Just imagine using up all your energy to get a message across, only for your listener to be confused when you're done. That's not communication. Communication isn't about you. You have something to say, that's cool. But you have to consider your listener.

It's clarity that aids understanding. This means that your choice of words should be at the listener's level not above them. Clarity also goes along with empathy. Another communication skill. Putting yourself in your listeners shoes makes you understand their comprehension level and how they'll feel when you say certain things to them.

During conversations, what are you doing when you're not talking? Listening, right? But not all of us do it well. To build healthy relationships, you need to learn to listen more than you talk.

Listen to the words the other person says. Listen to what they're not saying with words. Listen to the tone of their voice and their mood while talking. Be an active listener. That's how to really understand their message.

Gestures are also ways of communication. Pay attention to that, too. How do you feel when someone seems distracted when you're talking to them? I know that feeling. It's not usually a pleasant one.

Don't do it to people. That might mark the end of your conversation with that person. You'll just notice that they're not telling you things again. They want to, but they know when they do, you don't listen, so why try? Such attitudes make relationships sore.

CONFLICT RESOLUTION

The scenario I painted in the previous section could lead to conflict. When you begin to notice sudden changes in the behavior of your partner without any explanation, something is wrong.

They might start acting distant. They can withdraw themselves, or feel irritated when you're around. It's a sign of a brewing conflict. Like I said previously, when you notice that your partner doesn't want to talk to you like before, a conflict is on.

Arguments, constant blame, criticism, and tense atmosphere are also indications of an ongoing conflict. When you're getting silent treatments from your partner, you should not go to bed with your two eyes closed. Ha! That's figurative, though.

When this happens, what do you do?

The moment you realize what's going on, just come out straight. Don't accuse your partner of anything, like saying, "What's wrong with you? You've been staying away for a while." That could make their defensive walls go higher.

Before you even think of saying anything after you've noticed the signs, create a friendly atmosphere, maybe a hangout or just an evening together in a serene environment. You could even go for a movie.

Your objective is to create a safe environment for that conversation to hold. The tension will also be reduced in such an atmosphere. Then you can talk about your observations. They'll be willing to open up.

When they're talking, you should empathize with them. See things from their perspective. Don't try to be defensive or justify anything. If they blame you for it, accept it first. If there's a need to clarify anything after they blamed you, do it gently without raising your voice or accusing them in return.

Apologize and assure them that you'll ensure such things that led to the conflict won't repeat itself. However, you should also know that conflicts are normal in relationships. Instead of seeing them as negative and unresolvable, you should view them as opportunities to strengthen your relationship and grow.

RELEASING RESENTMENT FOR INNER PEACE

Conflicts can lead to resentment. When negative feelings aren't addressed, negative emotions like anger, hurt, and frustration can accumulate over time. This can produce feelings of resentment towards your partner.

Another thing that can cause resentment in relationships is when your partner isn't listening or taking your concerns seriously. You may start to feel resentful towards them.

When resentment grows in relationships, it makes you blame your partner for things that aren't their fault. The more you do this, the more angry you get with them. In that context, trust will be lost.

You might think that it'll stop there, but it can also impact other areas of your life as well, like your work and friendship. You'll lose your peace and always have a stream of negativity pulsing through your mind.

The primary key to releasing resentment is to first let go of every negative thoughts and emotions you have towards that person. It's your thoughts about them that keeps fueling your resentment towards them. You can't feel otherwise if you don't root out those thoughts.

You didn't do it for them, you did it for yourself first. If you keep holding on to those thoughts and feelings, it'll have impacts on your mental and physical health. It's just a matter of time.

Now, you have to identify what caused the resentment. Conflicts or lack of good communication are just a few. There are others. So, you have to find out what caused the resentment.

Discuss it with your partner. Trying using "I" statements, like "I feel resentful when you do ____." It might not be a deliberate action by your partner. But after calling their attention to it, they'll understand your view.

Be forgiven and understanding as well. A relationship is the coming together of two imperfect people. They try to build something lasting together. While doing that they might step on each other's toes. It's normal. But that shouldn't end the relationship.

BUILDING TRUST

When you start a relationship with someone, you may have some positive emotional feelings towards them. But emotions are transient. Relationships are not built on emotions.

One of the things that really determines the longevity of any relationship is trust. And I can tell you that it's not built in a day. Different factors contribute to what makes people trust each other in relationships.

Trust is a product of consistency in character. Don't be too quick to trust people. Some folks are so good at masking their true personality. They might hide their true intentions just to get your attention and win your trust.

Don't fall prey. Give them time. Time is a revealer. Someone who's faking their character will eventually slip up with time. This also implies that if you want people to trust you in relationships, you need to be consistent in your character.

And do you know what? Consistency in character is a product of honesty and being true to who you are. When you try to portray who you're not to your partner, you'll be forced to keep up the act. How long will you do that for?

Trust is also built when you prove yourself to be reliable. Your partner needs to be sure that you won't disappoint them. If you have a track record of lateness, failing on promises, and giving excuses, you won't be trusted on anything serious.

Don't say what you can't do. Don't try to impress. Just be yourself.

SETTING HEALTHY BOUNDARIES IN RELATIONSHIPS

Just like I stated previously, boundaries are one of the things that guards against toxicity in relationships.

Boundaries are like protective shields that help to keep out unhealthy behaviors and maintain the integrity of your relationship. They also serve as expectations that define roles in relationships.

So, from the onset, it's right to communicate what is acceptable and what is not with your partner. There are behaviors you might not condone, the same thing goes for them.

Boundaries clear out assumptions. They create a sense of safety and stability in relationships. This is what fosters emotional connection and deeper trust.

Boundaries aren't just about saying "no." They're also about setting healthy limits for yourself. It's also about showing respect for your own needs and values. This helps prevent resentment and burnout in your relationship.

When setting your boundaries, be honest with yourself about the things you can tolerate and things you can't. And when you're communicating them to your partner, be assertive. Be firm but respectful.

But then, you're not the only one permitted to have boundaries in a relationship. Your partner can also have theirs. Know theirs too and respect it. That's the basis for trust and mutual understanding.

THE ROLE OF VULNERABILITY IN AUTHENTIC CONNECTION

Can you stand completely naked before a stranger? Well, that's definitely an illogical thing to do, right? How about you telling someone you're just meeting every important detail about your life? That too is illogical.

Just as you can't do any of the above with a stranger, you can't be vulnerable with a stranger as well. So, before talking about vulnerability, you must have a level of close relationship with the person. In this case, your partner.

Also, the issue of trust should have been settled before thinking of vulnerability. So, being vulnerable is about letting your guard down. It's also about being honest about your feelings, and sharing your authentic self with your partner.

When you're vulnerable, you're opening up and allowing yourself to be seen as you are. This is what creates a deep level of intimacy and understanding. It allows you to be loved for who you truly are—flaws and all else.

When you're vulnerable with your partner, they also respond with empathy and acceptance. Your relationship is bound to grow stronger with time. But then, don't forget that it has to be with someone you trust and in a safe environment.

Case Study

Meg spent most of her life as a people pleaser. To her, the approval and acceptance of others were like oxygen, essential to her self-worth and happiness. She'd drop everything for anyone.

She would drown in emotional labor to make sure she was everyone's 'go-to.' And with each successful act of pleasing, she felt special, irreplaceable, and needed. But then, no matter how many people she helped, the approval she got never lasted.

Eventually, she hit rock bottom. She thought she wasn't valuable anymore. She declined into darkness. It was later she realized that she had been seeking validation in all the wrong places.

WORKBOOK 7

1. How do you rate yourself on the communication skills on a scale of 1-5

Clarity: _____

Active Listening: _____

Empathy: _____

2. Which of the three skills needs more attention for you?

_____

_____

_____

_____

Mention 3 ways you'll develop this skill:

1. _____
2. _____
3. _____

TAKEAWAY 7

- Toxic relationships are costly. Their ultimate price is usually your happiness and fulfillment. Toxic relationships take more from you than you receive. The best decision to make is to let it go.
- Trust is a determinant factor for the longevity of any relationship. With consistency of character and the quality of being reliable, you can win the trust of your partner.

When we understand that life can't be lived in isolation, we make efforts to build healthy relationships, and even intimate ones. Considering the risk that comes with being in relationships with the wrong persons, this chapter has created every basic guide needed to have great relationships.

And to the final step of this insightful adventure, how do we ensure the changes you've experienced aren't transient? How do we have a long lasting peace? Those are questions I'll answer in the next chapter.

8

LASTING CHANGE FOR LASTING PEACE

The secret of making lasting change is to acknowledge and accept that real change takes time and patience.

— DANA ARCURI

Every chapter of this book was geared towards helping you experience mental transformation. But transformation isn't total if you don't know how to sustain it.

A good medical doctor usually tells you what to do after you recover from an ailment, right? Well, as your tour guide on this transformational journey, here's my final counsel.

SETTING REALISTIC EXPECTATIONS

One of the primary reasons for negative thoughts is when people fail at something. Are they meant to fail? Not necessarily. But sometimes, their expectation was above what they could do.

When people set unrealistic expectations, they're bound to fail. When they do, it opens the door for negative thoughts and feelings. They did that to themselves.

There's a fine line between dreaming big and setting attainable expectations. When we set unrealistic expectations, we're setting ourselves up for disappointment. That's where there's a basic principle for setting goals - SMART.

Be specific about what you want to achieve. Have a yardstick for measuring when you've achieved that goal. Your goal should be achievable. It should be relevant with your values and vision. Then set a time for your goals.

Let your expectations from people also be minimal. Don't assume that no one can hurt you. Even the closest person to you can. Aren't they human? Humans are bound to err. So, create an allowance in your heart for people to make mistakes. When they do, the pain won't be much and it'll be easier to forgive them.

BUILDING HABITS FOR SUCCESS

When you wrote an entrance exam and you passed, did it happen by luck? I doubt it. Or when you got a promotion at work, did you pay for it? I'm sure the system doesn't work that way.

You certainly did some things that led to the successes you've recorded in your life till this point. Those things are habits.

Habits are the building blocks of success. They might be small, daily actions. But they add up to create big results over time. To avoid failing consistently, you can build habits for success. Habits stick.

But forming new habits isn't always easy, yeah? It takes patience, commitment, and discipline to form habits that stick. In essence, your life can be a chronicle of successes at different phases.

How do we do this?

Start small. Build our habit gradually by starting with a small action. Then do it regularly. Ensure you make it fun so that you don't get discouraged. It doesn't have to be rigorous and hard.

When building a new habit, it's helpful if you have someone you're accountable to. You can also use some devices like habit trackers to track your progress. What matters is your commitment and consistency.

But like I stated, you have to be patient. The results will come. Just stay committed. Before long, you'll realize that you do those habits subconsciously.

OVERCOMING SETBACKS AND RELAPSES

Success is beautiful and habits can help us experience it always. However, is it possible to always succeed without setbacks? There will be occasional experiences of setbacks.

When they happen how should you respond?

It's important for you to recognize that setbacks are part of the learning process too. You've learned EQ and a lot of techniques on how to control the traffic of thoughts in your mind.

When setbacks occur or when you relapse, how you respond is an indication of how much you've learned and mastered during your transformational experiences. Will you bounce back or stay down?

The primary thing is never to allow setbacks stop you from reaching your ultimate goal. If you keep rising every time you fall, you're showing strength and resilience. That's powerful.

Remember that setbacks are not indications that you're a failure. NO! It's just a chance for you to pause, reflect, and re-plan your course. I know that setbacks can be hard to deal with. However, with patience and a supportive community, you can bounce back.

All through the process, ensure you maintain a growth mindset. This mindset will help you see setbacks as another opportunity to grow. Stay positive throughout the process.

FINDING BALANCE AND SELF-CARE

Perry (2022) shared a mind blowing stats about the American society before the 2020 global pandemic. She stated that a staggering 67% of Americans prioritized the needs of others. They often felt guilty when they carved out time for self-care.

Yet, a full 68% of those respondents yearned for more time to focus on themselves. Whether it's work, family obligations, or your never-ending to-do lists, self-care often gets pushed to the bottom.

But maintaining a healthy work-life balance isn't just about clocking out on time. It's about taking those precious moments to nourish your mind, body, and soul.

Do you check up on yourself like you do to others?

Do you spend time with yourself like you do for others?

Do you encourage and strengthen yourself like you do for others?

Do you pour into yourself the same way you do for others?

Do you care for yourself with the same tenderness and devotion that you extend to others?

Or are you constantly on the giving end?

Friend, you have to be the priority. That's not selfishness! Self-care isn't a luxury. It's a necessity you can't do without.

According to the Empowerment Counseling Associates (n.d.), self-help isn't a one-off exercise. It's a way of life. It's a daily practice that helps you survive different phases of life.

It's a commitment to yourself. It's a devotion to your physical, mental, and spiritual well-being. And you keep doing this no matter what life throws at you. Get enough sleep whenever you need to.

Setting boundaries is also part of self-care. Regularly exercising is also a form of self-care. Anything you do to care for your well-being is your self-care.

Case Study

Jolie was a powerhouse in the corporate world. At just 28, she'd already climbed to the top of the ladder at a prominent Canadian company. But the cost of success took a toll on her.

To secure and maintain her position, she worked 16 to 20 hours a day. She was never stopping for a break. She sacrificed sleep, leisure, and weekends. Her life became a relentless race against the clock.

Her relentless drive pushed her to the brink of disaster. Before reaching 30, Jolie suffered a life threatening stroke, collapsing under the weight of her own ambition.

Did you know that someone had to fill Jolie's position in the company after that incident? Work didn't stop, but she did. Prioritize your self-care. Else, everything else will move on without you.

CELEBRATING PROGRESS

You've put so much effort and resources into arriving where you are now. Who else deserves some shout out? You!

Don't shy away from celebrating those little wins. You accomplish your tasks over a course of time. Celebrate it. You're beginning to see changes in your behavioral and emotional responses, celebrate it.

The emphasis of this celebration isn't on the results per se, it's those seemingly insignificant progress. Acknowledge your hard work because it's yielding some results already.

When you celebrate your progress, it propels you forward. It keeps you motivated to forge ahead. It also builds confidence in you. Recognizing your own achievements builds your self-esteem. Can you see the ripple effect?

Celebrating your progress is another way of building resilience within. You're better equipped to handle setbacks when you learn to appreciate your own progress. You can start celebrating your wins by giving yourself a treat for reaching a milestone.

You can also share your success. Tell you friends or loved ones about your progress. Receiving positive feedback from them can motivate you to keep going. Journaling your progress is also a great way to celebrate your progress.

LIVING A LIFE OF PURPOSE AND FULFILLMENT

In the previous part, there was an elaborate talk on living purposefully. It's worth saying here again that the best way to sustain transformation is by living a life of meaning.

Living with purpose is the bedrock of lasting changes. It gives you a sense of direction and provides motivation for the long drive. Purposeful living isn't just going through the motions.

When you combine purposeful living with celebrating progress, you create a powerful cycle of growth and fulfillment. When you're living a purposeful life, you start to see things differently. More positively I'd say.

Instead of focusing on what you lack, you'll start to appreciate what you have. You'll see opportunities where you once saw obstacles. The key is to identify what matters most to you. Then let your actions and decisions agree with your values.

You'd be creating a powerful force the universe would have to reckon with. Just stay on course. It's a process. However, it's one that can lead to a deeply fulfilling meaningful existence.

WORKBOOK 8

1. Identify 2 things that serve as setbacks for you.

1. _____

2. _____

2. How do these setbacks affect your goals and well-being?

1. _____

2. _____

3. How can you transform the setbacks into opportunities for growth?

_____

_____

_____

_____

TAKEAWAY 8

- The SMART technique of drawing goals isn't cliche. Having unrealistic expectations from yourself is what causes the waves of disappointment and negativity. SMART technique can halt that wave.
- Never expect to experience growth on a long term when you're not committed to taking care of yourself. Making a habit of caring for yourself daily is a guarantee for a happy life daily.

CONCLUSION

I've heard people say that everything that has a beginning has an end. Well, that's quite true of this book. This is the part where I get to wind down. But then, did you also know that when a thing ends, it gives way for a new beginning?

Yes! The end of this book gives way to a new beginning for you. It's a new beginning for you, dear reader. This is where you begin to talk about your story of transformation. And if you may, document it and get others to hear about it.

Just like I shared with you, more people need to know what you learned about the science behind negative thoughts. Their sources and how they thrive in our minds. You should also let people know how they disrupted your inner peace.

You can also share your personal transformational experiences from when you began to break the cyclical negative patterns of emotions, thoughts, and behavior with techniques like mindfulness and CBT.

There's also the part where you began to gain control over your emotions through EQ skills. You became more aware of your emotions, thoughts, and actions. That awareness helped you to regulate that triad better. So, you're not like a pawn on a chessboard.

If breaking the cycle of negativity was all we did, the book wouldn't have completed its work. Ending a thing creates a vacuum for something else to fill up the space. In this case, that space had to be filled with positivity through positive psychology.

To sustain the progress and changes you've started to experience during our journey together, I told you that it was necessary for you to have a growth mindset and have a vision for living.

This will help you to be resilient when you experience setbacks and it'll help you to live a more meaningful life. All this adds up to make you live happily daily regardless of the circumstances. And you'll experience inner peace regularly even in the midst of chaos.

It's been a great delight to have guided you through this transformational experience. The ultimate isn't to quieten your mind, rather it's to achieve inner peace.

I look forward to hearing your thoughts and, perhaps, reading your stories too. You can share them as reviews of this book.

Have a great time living peacefully and happily always.

REFERENCES

American Psychological Association. (2018, April 19). *APA Dictionary of Psychology.* Dictionary.apa.org. https://dictionary.apa.org/cognitive-distortion

Helou, M. (2023, October 17). *The Art of Mindfulness: Cultivating Inner Peace.* Www.linkedin.com. https://www.linkedin.com/pulse/art-mindfulness-cultivating-inner-peace-monique-helou-2wilf/

Robinson, J. (2021, September 21). *Self Awareness: The key to know your inner world and heal yourself.* PACEs-Connection. https://www.pacesconnection.com/blog/self-awareness-the-key-to-know-your-inner-world-and-heal-yourself

Rose, H. (2022, April 28). *The psychology of negative*

thinking. Ness Labs. https://nesslabs.com/negative-thinking

Rumination: Stuck In The Cycle Of Negative Thinking. (2023, June 23). Novum Psychiatry. https://novumpsychiatry.com/blog/rumination-negative-thinking/

Xi, J., & Lee, M. T. (2021). Inner Peace as a Contribution to Human Flourishing. *Measuring Well-Being*, 435–481. https://doi.org/10.1093/oso/9780197512531.003.0016

Ackerman, C. E. (2018, April 20). *What is Positive Psychology & Why is It Important? [2020 Update].* Positive-Psychology.com. https://positivepsychology.com/what-is-positive-psychology-definition/#founder-positive-psychology

Andrade, G. (2019). The ethics of positive thinking in healthcare. *Journal of Medical Ethics and History of Medicine,* *12*(18). https://doi.org/10.18502/jmehm.v12i18.2148

Bethune, S. (2023). *APA Poll Reveals Toxic workplaces, Other Significant Workplace Mental Health Challenges.* Apa.org. https://www.apa.org/news/press/releases/2023/07/work-mental-health-challenges

Cherry, K. (2023a, May 4). *The Power of Positive*

Thinking. Verywell Mind. https://www.verywellmind. com/what-is-positive-thinking-2794772

Cherry, K. (2023b, December 31). *5 Key Components of Emotional Intelligence*. Verywell Mind. https://www.very wellmind.com/components-of-emotional-intelligence-2795438

Gitau, P. (2023, March 16). *LinkedIn Login, Sign in.* LinkedIn. https://www.linkedin.com/pulse/5-compo nents-emotional-intelligence-understanding-key-gitau/

Johns Hopkins Medicine. (2019). *The Power of Positive Thinking*. Johns Hopkins Medicine Health Library. https://www.hopkinsmedicine.org/health/wellness-and-prevention/the-power-of-positive-thinking

Marschall, A. (2021, December 13). *What to Know About Strengths-Based Therapy*. Verywell Mind. https://www. verywellmind.com/strengths-based-therapy-defini tion-and-techniques-5211679

Peterson, C. (2008, May 16). *What Is Positive Psychology, and What Is It Not?* Psychology Today. https://www. psychologytoday.com/us/blog/the-good-life/200805/ what-is-positive-psychology-and-what-is-it-not

Schimelpfening, N. (2024, January 16). *How Mindful-ness-Based Cognitive Therapy Works*. Verywell Mind.

https://www.verywellmind.com/mindfulness-based-cognitive-therapy-1067396#:~:text=Mindfulness%2D-based%20cognitive%20thera-py%20(MBCT)%20is%20a%20type%20of

Villines, Z. (2021, October 25). *Behavioral activation: How it works, examples, and more.* Www.medicalnewstoday.com. https://www.medicalnewstoday.com/articles/behavioral-activation

Xie, H. (2013). Strengths-based approach for mental health recovery. *Iranian Journal of Psychiatry and Behavioral Sciences, 7*(2), 5–10. https://www.ncbi.nlm.nih.gov/pmc/articles/PMC3939995/

Clarke, J. (2022, April 22). *What Is Analysis Paralysis?* Verywell Mind. https://www.verywellmind.com/what-is-analysis-paralysis-5223790

Perry, E. (2022, September 10). *Self-Care and Work-Life Balance: How to Take Care of Yourself.* Www.betterup.com. https://www.betterup.com/blog/self-care-and-work-life-balance

Self Care Is The Key To Finding Your Balance. (n.d.). Empowerment Counseling Associates. http://www.counselingtoempower.com/self-care.html

Made in the USA
Las Vegas, NV
12 October 2024

96706798R20115